Travel Arizona II

A GUIDE TO THE BEST TOURS AND SITES

TEXT
LEO W. BANKS, TOM DOLLAR
ROSE HOUK, SAM NEGRI, JOE STOCKER

PHOTOGRAPHS
ARIZONA HIGHWAYS CONTRIBUTORS

PHOTOGRAPHY EDITOR
RICHARD MAACK

DESIGN AND PRODUCTION
VICKY SNOW

PRODUCTION COORDINATOR – SECOND PRINTING
KIM ENSENBERGER

MAPS
KEVIN J. KIBSEY

PHOENIX & TUCSON MAPS
COURTESY QWEST DEX

COPY EDITOR
EVELYN HOWELL

BOOK EDITOR
BOB ALBANO

ARIZONA HIGHWAYS
BOOKS

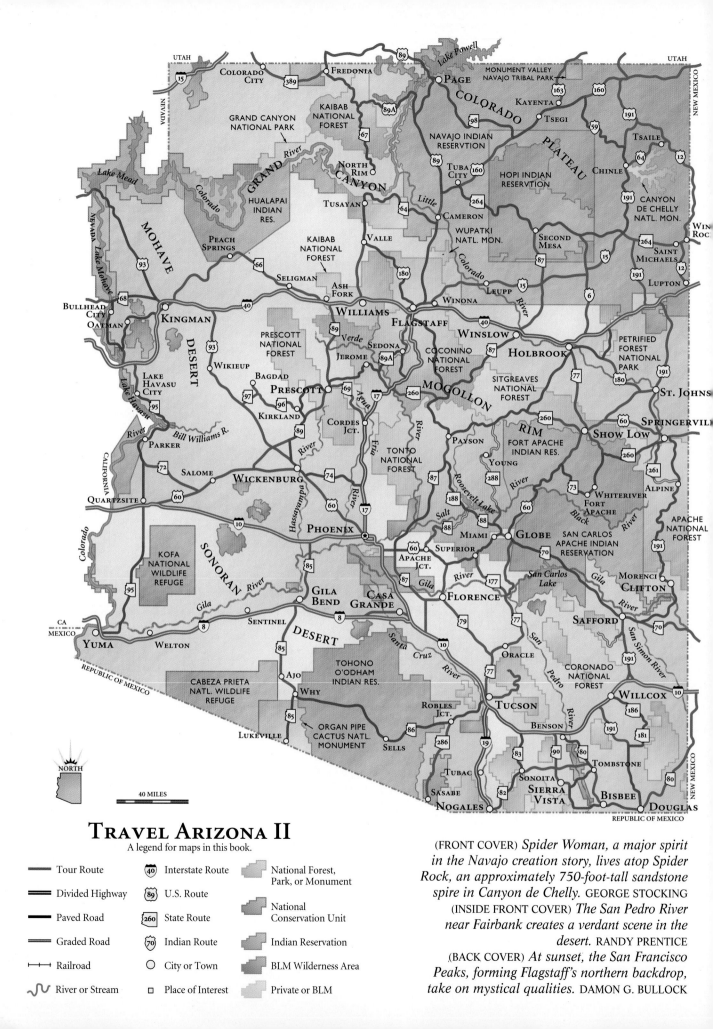

TRAVEL ARIZONA II

A legend for maps in this book.

- ——— Tour Route
- ═══ Divided Highway
- ▬▬▬ Paved Road
- ═══ Graded Road
- ├──┤ Railroad
- ∿∿ River or Stream

- (40) Interstate Route
- (89) U.S. Route
- (260) State Route
- (70) Indian Route
- ○ City or Town
- □ Place of Interest

- National Forest, Park, or Monument
- National Conservation Unit
- Indian Reservation
- BLM Wilderness Area
- Private or BLM

NORTH

40 MILES

Travel Arizona II

A GUIDE TO THE BEST TOURS AND SITES

CONTENTS

Introduction **6**

Index **158**

NORTHERN

Touring Flagstaff and the High Country VISITING THE PAST ALONG THE WAY **8**

The Grand Canyon, Ruins, and Volcanoes A LOOP TRIP FROM FLAGSTAFF **16**

High Desert Navajo and Hopi Country ANCIENT SITES, GEOLOGIC WONDERS **24**

From Lake Powell to the North Rim and Pipe Spring ADVENTURING IN THE ARIZONA STRIP **32**

CENTRAL

Natural Beauty and Small Town Charm RIM COUNTRY TO THE PAINTED DESERT **40**

A Pleasant Lesson on Arizona's Diversity DESERT TO MOUNTAINS TO MEADOWS **48**

A Trail Back Through Time SEDONA, PRESCOTT, AND VERDE VALLEY **56**

A Short Trip Through the Centuries HISTORICAL SITES AND ANCIENT RUINS **66**

WESTERN

Along the Lower Colorado River YUMA AND WILDLIFE REFUGES **72**

Roaming Along the Colorado River AN ECLECTIC MIX OF ATTRACTIONS **78**

Where the Old West Meets the Water HISTORIC ROUTE 66 AND LAKE MEAD **84**

A Sonoran Desert Sojourn IN THE FOOTSTEPS OF EXPEDITIONS **90**

SOUTHERN

The Cochise Circle WHERE FACT AND FOLKLORE MINGLE **96**

Touring Along Deadmen's Highway FROM TUCSON TO THE BORDER AT NOGALES **104**

Getting Acquainted with the Old Pueblo TUCSON REFLECTS THREE CULTURES **112**

Outdoors in Tucson HIKES, BIKES, AND THE LIKE **120**

PHOENIX AREA

Getting Acquainted with Central Phoenix ENJOYING DOWNTOWN AND NEARBY AREAS **128**

Getting Acquainted with the Valley FOCUSING ON THE AREA'S UNIQUENESS **138**

The Valley's Urban Outdoors STAYING CLOSE WHILE YOU GET OUT **146**

Indian Heritage PRE-HISTORY AND MODERN CULTURES **152**

Published by the Book Division of *Arizona Highways* magazine, a monthly publication of the Arizona Department of Transportation, 2039 West Lewis Avenue, Phoenix, Arizona 85009.　　Telephone: (602) 712-2200　　Web site: www.arizonahighways.com

Win Holden — Publisher　　　　　　　Bob Albano — Managing Editor　　　Evelyn Howell, P.K. McMahon — Associate Editors
Peter Ensenberger — Director of Photography　　Mary Winkelman Velgos — Art Director　　Cindy Mackey — Production Director

　　Printed in Hong Kong.　　Library of Congress Catalog Number 98-87497　　ISBN 0-916179-80-X

Introduction

Watch a sunset from a serene Grand Canyon overlook or ride the rails through countryside teeming with Old West history and scenery or stroll through a wildlife refuge.

Mix with the townfolks of Flagstaff at a down-home eatery or enjoy home-made pie at a cafe in the pines at Strawberry or have lunch at Cafe Sage on a complex built by missionaries on the Navajo Reservation.

Walk the floors and examine the wares of a famed trading post established by John Lorenzo Hubbell, whose career began in 1878 and who came to be known as "Double Glasses" and "Old Mexican." But for really old, visit the mesas where the Hopi people have lived for at least a thousand years.

With *Travel Arizona II*, historic, cultural, scenic, and otherwise fascinating sites of Arizona unfold for you. This guidebook highlights the best that Arizona offers through the efforts of five veteran writers — with nearly 150 years of exploring this state — more than three dozen photographers, and specialists in research, maps, and book design.

Succeeding *Travel Arizona*, this all-new volume has been expanded from 128 to 160 pages. Included are 14 trips in all regions of the state, plus three chapters devoted to the best attractions in Phoenix and Tucson, two chapters devoted to the "urban outdoors" of Phoenix and of Tucson, and a chapter highlighting sites and institutions focusing on ancient and contemporary Native American cultures.

Included are the names and telephone numbers of contacts that can give you more information on hours of operation, admission fees, special events, and directions.

We've also included some Internet Web sites, starting with three that feature links covering all aspects of travel in Arizona. Our own *Arizona Highways* Web site (*www.arizonahighways.com*) links you to sites brimming

with information about Arizona's communities, national parks and forests, state parks, cowboy lore, Native Americans, museums, cultural and historical attractions, archaeology, outdoor recreation, observatories, and geology.

The second useful Web site (*www.arizonaguide.com*) is the official site of the Arizona Office of Tourism. It offers a calendar-of-events feature and links related to travel and vacations.

Covering the entire region north of Phoenix, the third site (*www.tripusa.com/arizona/*) is a cooperative effort among the Arizona Department of Transportation, the I-40 Corridor Coalition, and Castle Rock Services. Its links include road and weather conditions, lodging, and activities.

The authors have written many articles for *Arizona Highways* as well as other guidebooks. Let's meet them.

Leo W. Banks has lived and traveled throughout Arizona for 25 years. He now considers the state his home, and relishes opportunities to explore new places, especially those tied to the region's history. His advice to travelers is to bring water, a cell phone, a hat, and plenty of chips.

Tom Dollar guides you over western Arizona and an area of southeastern Arizona especially rich in history and scenery. He authored two previous *Arizona Highways* guidebooks: *Indian Country* and *Tucson to Tombstone*.

Sam Negri is a journalist whose work for two major Arizona daily newspapers has taken him to all parts of Arizona. He co-authored *Travel Arizona: The Back Roads*.

Rose Houk worked for two years as a park ranger at the Grand Canyon. Her experience is reflected in chapters on the Grand Canyon, Flagstaff and nearby areas, and Navajo-Hopi country. Her books include *The Peaks*, (a guide to northern Arizona published by *Arizona Highways*); *An Introduction to Grand Canyon Ecology*; and *Guide to the South Kaibab Trail*.

Joe Stocker, although in his 80s, remains an avid bicyclist, riding nearly every day. He's been writing about Arizona attractions for nearly a half century. The author of the original *Travel Arizona,* he urges Arizona travelers to get the most from their trips by stopping often, looking, pondering, and making a personal connection with the attributes of each site.

— *Bob Albano* ▼

(PRECEDING PANEL, PAGES 4-5) *Besides its namesake plant, Organ Pipe Cactus National Monument displays fiery ocotillo and golden brittlebush.* RANDY PRENTICE
(LEFT) *One of Arizona's grandest sights is sunset at the Grand Canyon — this one's at Mather Point on the South Rim.* ROBERT G. McDONALD
(ABOVE) *Riders wind through the Superstitions.* TOM BEAN

Touring Flagstaff and the High Country

VISITING THE PAST ALONG THE WAY

by Rose Houk

Over his lunch hour, the young lawyer leaves his shoes with the shoeshine man. Shod in a pair of courtesy house slippers, he shuffles across San Francisco Street to Martan's Burrito Palace. There, Miss Alice serves up the day's special, a plate loaded with enchiladas, beans, rice, and all the trimmings.

This street scene is essence of Flagstaff, a highly eclectic town with eateries like Martan's, whose unfussy facade reveals little of the community camaraderie within. Here people of all professions — lawyers, river guides, ambulance drivers, artists, students, construction workers —gather for some of the best Mexican food in town, served with a smile and no pretensions.

Then there's Miss Alice. Everybody calls her that, and everybody thanks her personally as they leave Martan's. Her full name is Alice Flemons, and she's an institution in Flagstaff. Granddaughter of a freed slave, she came to northern Arizona from Louisiana in 1953. She and her husband, who worked for the Saginaw Lumber Mill, lived on the south side. For many years, Miss Alice took care of her mother, Eugenia Holbert. When *Arizona Daily Sun* reporter Paul Sweitzer interviewed Mrs. Holbert in 1983, she was 112 and still quilting, taking care of her great-grandchild, and learning to read. She died at age 118.

Though Miss Alice's native Southern tastes tend toward corn bread, collard greens, and sweet potato pie, she recalls learning to cook Mexican food in Flagstaff in 1968. She retired a few years back, but returned to work when Gloria and Jerry Korkki reopened Martan's on North San Francisco Street.

Did she ever have trouble adapting to Flagstaff? Sipping an orange drink during a rare break from the stove, Miss Alice shakes her head and laughs: "I love Flagstaff, I got so many friends here." (Not to mention five grandchildren and 10 great-grandchildren who keep her plenty busy when she's not cooking).

Flagstaff came to town status in 1882 with the arrival

Towns & sites: Flagstaff, Walnut Canyon National Monument, Meteor Crater, Homolovi Ruins State Park, Coconino National Forest, Mormon Lake, and Lake Mary.

Overview: On this loop trip, you'll visit the bustling college and tourist town of Flagstaff, ancient Indian dwelling sites, a huge meteorite crater, and high-country forest and lakes.

Routes & mileage: About 200 miles total. Take Interstate 40 east from Flagstaff for 10 miles to Exit 204 and drive south two miles to Walnut Canyon National Monument. Return to I-40 and drive east for 29 miles to Exit 233 and go south for six miles to Meteor Crater and Museum. Back on I-40, go 24 miles east to Exit 257 and go two miles north on State Route 87 to Homolovi Ruins State Park. From the park, go south on State 87 through Winslow for 50 miles to Clints Well. Turn right (north) on Forest Service Road 3 to Happy Jack, Mormon Lake, Lake Mary, and back to Flagstaff, 55 miles.

Time to allow: One long day, or overnight at Winslow or Mormon Lake Lodge.

(LEFT) *Often called the Peaks, the San Francisco Mountains, shown here with an autumn dusting of snow, form a distinctive backdrop for Flagstaff.* DAVID MUENCH
(ABOVE, RIGHT) *A bicyclist seeking serenity pedals over Hart Prairie near Flagstaff.* MIKE PADIAN
(RIGHT) *Community camaraderie thrives in coffee houses like this one in downtown Flagstaff.* STEWART AITCHISON

of the Atlantic & Pacific Railroad. Railroading, ranching, and logging nourished the mountain town's economic roots for decades.

Downtown has undergone a metamorphosis in the last several years — many layers of plaster, stucco, and fake fronts have been peeled back to reveal original, turn-of-the-century red sandstone, brick walls, tin ceilings, and glass fronts. Inside, though, the businesses are modern: coffee houses, microbreweries, backcountry outfitters, and galleries. Flagstaff is now a small city focused to a great degree on tourists, who come from all over the world on their way to the Grand Canyon.

(LEFT) *Railroad tracks, old Route 66 (in front of the depot), and the San Francisco Peaks comprise three of the ingredients flavoring Flagstaff.*
(OPPOSITE PAGE) *Northern Arizona University (its Old Main is pictured) contributes to the activity and cultural mix from which Flagstaff draws its essence.*
BOTH BY DAMON G. BULLOCK
(ABOVE) *Visitors can tour Lowell Observatory on Mars Hill, the site from which the planet Pluto was discovered.*
RICHARD MAACK

With a healthy cultural and scientific mix, beautiful natural setting, and tenacious outdoor ethic, Flagstaff attracts many urban refugees. It's an active town — there's always something going on. A check of the weekly entertainment rag lists activities such as stargazing at Lowell Observatory, exhibits at the Museum of Northern Arizona, a musical performance at Northern Arizona University, a plant sale at the Arboretum, dancing, literary readings, happy hours, and a country band at the venerable Museum Club on old Route 66. Summer brings an outdoor festival clogging the streets with visitors up escaping from desert heat or on their way to the Grand Canyon.

Winter draws the snow-loving crowd for alpine and Nordic skiing, snowboarding, snowmobiling, and dogsledding.

Flagstaff serves as a base for trips into a million acres of surrounding forest, mountains, and national parks. One is Walnut Canyon National Monument, 10 miles east. This heavily treed limestone canyon was once home to a people that archaeologists call the Sinagua. These prehistoric farmers lived on the rims of Walnut Canyon and built some 300 rooms in natural alcoves in the canyon's cliff walls.

Walnut Canyon was most densely populated between A.D. 1150 and 1220, though the Sinagua were living all around the area earlier and into the next century.

The Sinagua grew corn, beans, and squash in fields on the mesa tops. They guarded their valuable produce by erecting small houses near their fields where they stayed during the growing season. They also built walled structures on high promontories. Within the walls of Walnut Canyon there are five of these so-called "forts," which probably were lookouts or places where access to the canyon could be controlled and the community protected.

One of the first questions visitors ask is: How did the Sinagua get in and out of the steep-walled canyon? Park Service rangers point to natural breaks in the cliffs' faces where these mobile people, shod in yucca sandals, followed trails from their canyon homes to the rims.

When visitors learn that Sinagua means "without water," a fitting name for people who inhabited a dry region, their second question is: How did they get water? They got it from springs, rock depressions that briefly hold water after rain, and from the creek bed below, which may have flowed more than it does today. The Sinagua also made huge *ollas*, pottery jugs in which they gathered and stored water draining off the cliffs.

A wild garden for the prehistoric Sinagua, Walnut Canyon contained a rich diversity of edible and otherwise useful plants. A walk down the Island Trail will introduce you to this botanical wonderland — cactus and yucca on the warmer, drier, south-facing slopes; oaks and ferns in the wetter places. The Island Trail also brings you close to the cliff dwellings so you can peer into the small stone rooms, see where ancient fingers traced mortar joints, and where, year after year, hearth fires left layers of black soot on the walls.

Be aware, though, that the Island Trail drops 185 feet below the rim, with an equivalent climb back up steps to the rim. As an alternative, the flat, paved Rim Trail leads past typical pit house dwellings and affords beautiful views into the canyon.

At the turn of the 20th century, Walnut Canyon's location on the Atlantic & Pacific Railroad and the Ocean-to-Ocean Highway brought tourists — and looters. With little remorse, many of them walked off with a slew of artifacts, things that could have furnished amazing insights into the lives of the Sinagua. A few looters even resorted to dynamiting entire walls to get at the goods more easily. Outraged Flagstaff citizens won a campaign to have Walnut Canyon preserved as a national monument in 1915.

After you leave Walnut Canyon and drive about 20 miles east on Interstate 40, you'll come to Exit 230 for Two Guns. Once a popular stop for travelers on Route 66, Two Guns today features nothing more than a defunct gas station, tumbling rock ruins of a ghost town, and a sense of history.

A curse always seems to have shadowed Two Guns. Gunfights, stagecoach robberies, mysterious fires, and other mishaps have plagued various residents through the years. In the early 1990s, an optimistic new owner had plans to spiff up Two Guns, but those plans apparently never materialized.

About three miles north of I-40 on the road leading from Exit 230, lies Canyon Diablo, both a topographic feature and the name of a 19th-century rough-and-tumble, end-of-track railroad town. In its heyday, the town of Canyon Diablo was as wild as the West got. Its Hell Street boasted

(LEFT) *Prehistoric people lived in these cliff dwellings built between* A.D. *1125 and 1250 in what now is Walnut Canyon National Monument.* EDWARD McCAIN
(BELOW) *Meteor Crater pockmarks the Colorado Plateau (the San Francisco Peaks are on the horizon).*
(BELOW, RIGHT) *Homolovi Ruins State Park includes several ancient dwelling sites.* BOTH BY MICHAEL COLLIER

more than a dozen saloons, almost as many gambling houses, and a disproportionate number of brothels, two owned by women named Clabberfoot Annie and B.S. Mary. Population peaked at 2,000 in 1881-82, when the railroad awaited construction of a bridge that would span the 250-foot-deep canyon. (When the bridge finally arrived for installation, it was a few feet short of closing the span, causing a six-month delay in the railroad's westward progress.)

Discovery of some interesting rocks around Canyon Diablo inspired a protracted scientific debate concerning the true cause of the national landmark now known as Meteor Crater.

In 1886, a shepherd found in the vicinity lustrous, heavy pieces of rock that became known as the "Diablo irons." This find of iron-rich stone was reported to a group of scientists in 1891 as fragments of a meteorite. The existence nearby of a huge hole in the ground — Meteor Crater — was certainly known. Daniel Moreau Barringer believed the crater was caused by the impact of a meteorite. Barringer went head-to-head with prestigious scientist Grove Karl Gilbert, chief geologist for the U.S. Geological Survey, who thought the crater had volcanic origins.

Barringer spent the last 25 years of his life hoping to find the main mass of the meteorite body and to mine it. Remains of the central shaft in the bottom of the crater, and a shaft on the rim, can still be seen. Although Barringer's quest for mineral wealth was never realized, his ideas were finally vindicated. Scientists have shown that about 40,000 years ago, a powerful meteor hurled through Earth's atmosphere at about 40,000 miles an hour, struck this particular flat plain, and created a massive hole 560 feet deep and 4,000 feet across. The explosive force of the meteorite was equal to some 20 million tons of TNT. Most of the meteorite vaporized on impact, but fragments landed on the ground for miles around.

The Barringer family eventually leased the land to the Bar T Bar Ranch, which established the private Meteor Crater Enterprises to hold the famous landmark in public trust. Some 300,000 people a year pull off I-40 at Exit 233 and visit the crater and the museum perched on its rim. A series of beautiful oil paintings depicts the sequence of events from the moment of impact up to the present. Other audio and visual displays tell how Meteor Crater has led to an important understanding of impact features elsewhere on Earth, the moon, and other bodies in the solar system. In fact, several generations of Apollo astronauts trained at Meteor Crater before going to the moon, and their missions are commemorated in the museum's Astronaut Hall of Fame.

From well-placed windows inside the museum, you can gaze out at the awesome spectacle of the crater. Outside on the rocky rim, where the wind always blows unmitigated, you may accompany a guide on a 45-minute walk or simply view the various features of the crater from open-air platforms.

Falling stars figure prominently in oral histories of the Hopi, whose ancestors lived at what is now Homolovi Ruins State Park northeast of Meteor

Crater at I-40's Exit 257 (State Route 87). In the Hopi language, Homolovi means "place of the low mounds" for the isolated, colorful hills that rise from the valley of the Little Colorado River. Hopi history says that when they entered this, the Fourth World, they were instructed by Ma'saw to be stewards of the earth. During their migrations, they settled in certain places, cultivating the land and leaving "footprints" to mark their territory. Homolovi is one of those "footprints." Sighting a celestial sign, the Hopi left Homolovi around A.D. 1400, settling on the three mesas to the north where they still live today.

A good first stop is the park visitors center, where you'll gain an overview of the four major sites open to the public. Each is separated by several miles; you can drive to them, then follow trails that lead through the pueblos. Homolovi II, sprawling across the top of one hill, was a huge pueblo of some 800 rooms that once may have housed nearly a thousand people. Views of the colorful expanse of the Painted Desert are inspiring.

From the park, drive south on State 87 through the small railroad town of Winslow and continue south on the highway through a grassy piñon and juniper woodland. Now you're traveling in prime ranch and cattle land, the heart of the legendary Hashknife outfit, once one of the biggest spreads in the country.

The road climbs and swings west along the top of the Mogollon Rim and into the Blue Ridge District of the Coconino National Forest. At Clints Well, Forest Highway 3 leads north for the final leg of this trip, and you'll be in the midst of the largest continuous stand of ponderosa pine in the world.

Eventually the land opens out, giving a grand view of Mormon Lake, the largest natural lake in Arizona. It's shallow, though, and by late fall can be nearly dry. Dairy

Outdoor recreational opportunities abound in the area around Flagstaff all year long.
(BELOW, LEFT) *A hiker pauses in a field of alpine primrose in the San Francisco Peaks.*
(RIGHT) *An aspen forest near the Peaks provides an ideal autumn setting for a campsite.*
BOTH BY DAMON G. BULLOCK

and logging enterprises once operated beside the lake, but now most of the inhabitants are summer dwellers. For a good old time, stop at Mormon Lake Lodge for a fine steak dinner, complete with root-'em-toot-'em cowboys and country swing dancing. In winter, the lodge offers cross-country ski tours on groomed trails.

Just a few miles south of Flagstaff, Lake Mary, formed by a dam and providing part of the city's water supply, is a popular recreation spot.

All year long, the forest and the lakes are busy with boaters, anglers, hunters, campers, hikers, horseback riders, and bicyclists. From April through October, bird-watchers keep an eye out for ospreys, or "fish eagles," with wingspans up to six feet. Several pairs nest in ponderosa pine snags and live off the fish in the lakes. There is an osprey-viewing area just south of the Lake Mary Narrows Picnic Area. In winter, bald eagles arrive, lifting off from their tall perches and swooping down over the lakes for a fish or two. ◪

When You Go

Coconino National Forest: Happy Jack Information Center, (520) 477-2172. Mormon Lake Ranger District, (520) 774-1147. Supervisor's Office, Flagstaff, (520) 527-3600.

Flagstaff Chamber of Commerce & Visitor Center: (520) 774-9541 or (800) 842-7293.

Flagstaff Central Reservations: Free hotel reservation service for northern and central Arizona. (520) 527-8333 or (800) 527-8388.

Homolovi Ruins State Park: Winslow. (520) 289-4106. Admission fee. Campground/RV park. Web site: *www.pr.state.az.us/parkhtml/homolovi.html*

Lowell Observatory: (520) 774-3358, 774-2096 after hours. Admission fee. Tours, special presentations. Web site: *www.lowell.edu*

Meteor Crater: (800) 289-5898. Admission fee. Web site: *www.meteorcrater.com*

Mormon Lake Lodge: (520) 354-2227. Ask about cross-country ski touring with the Mormon Lake Ski Center.

Walnut Canyon National Monument: (520) 526-3367. Day-use area only. Admission fee. Web site: *www.nps.gov/waca/*

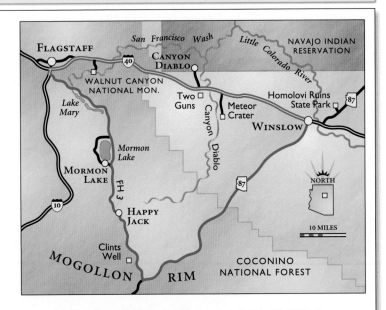

The Grand Canyon, Ruins, and Volcanoes

A LOOP TRIP FROM FLAGSTAFF

by Rose Houk

When I worked as a ranger on the South Rim of the Grand Canyon, visitors routinely would ask, "Where's the best place to see the Canyon?" That question always stumped me. I'd think about it for a minute, then have to admit I couldn't answer. To me, every viewpoint is different and every one is equally beautiful.

Nevertheless, I'd try to be helpful. Hopi Point out on the West Rim Drive is nice for sunset, but way too popular. (In my mind, a Grand Canyon sunset is best when it's a private experience.) From Mohave Point you can get a glimpse of the Colorado River, and on a good day even hear the muffled roar of Hermit Rapids a mile below. Then there's Grandview, out on the East Rim Drive, with a breathtaking vista of Vishnu Temple and Wotans Throne. And Lipan Point, where the Colorado River makes a big, sweeping curve around Unkar Delta. Sometimes you can spy little rubber rafts bouncing through the whitewater. Lipan is also a fantastic place to view hawks and other raptors migrating over the Canyon in the fall.

So, take your choice — and take your time. Wander a short distance away from any of the named points on the South Rim, find a rock a safe distance from the edge, and have a seat. Just soak in this grand spectacle, and contemplate the age of the rocks: older than mammals, older than dinosaurs, so old in places that no life at all is preserved in them.

Once you've sampled a few viewpoints, step down onto a trail and take a walk. It doesn't have to be a life's commitment, just a short walk, as far as you want to go, a mile or so down the Bright Angel or Kaibab trails. It's a different world down there, so quiet, so full of small things — flowers, squirrels, fossils. Coming back out, uphill all the way, you will begin to appreciate that this is indeed a very deep hole in the ground. And you may start to gain some perspective on humans' place amid this immensity of time and space.

To get to the South Rim, take U.S. 180 out of Flagstaff. This route, appropriately designated by Arizona as a scenic byway, climbs to about 8,000 feet elevation. Scribing the

Towns & sites: Flagstaff, the San Francisco Peaks, South Rim of the Grand Canyon, Desert View, Cameron, and Wupatki and Sunset Crater Volcano national monuments.

Overview: Beginning in Flagstaff you drive over one of Arizona's most scenic routes, viewing the state's highest mountains and arriving at its grandest canyon. The loop tour continues to an Indian trading post, Indian ruins, and volcanoes. As an option, you can drive from Flagstaff to Williams for a ride on a train to the Grand Canyon.

Routes & mileage: About 225 miles total. From Flagstaff take U.S. Route 180 north for 81 miles to the South Rim of the Grand Canyon. From Grand Canyon Village to Desert View on State Route 64 (also called East Rim Drive), it's 25 miles. From Desert View to Cameron, it's 33 miles on State 64. From Cameron to the Wupatki National Monument loop road, via U.S. Route 89, is 20 miles; the drive through the monument and back to U.S. 89 is 36 miles; and then it's about 15 miles to Flagstaff. From Flagstaff to Williams and the Grand Canyon Railway, it's 32 miles via Interstate 40.

Time to allow: Two to three days.

(LEFT) *A rainbow arches over O'Neill Butte, seen from Yavapai Point at the Grand Canyon.* RANDY PRENTICE
(ABOVE, RIGHT) *Bighorn sheep live on the Grand Canyon's rim and in its interior.* ED TOLIVER
(RIGHT) *Hikers descend the South Kaibab Trail for an intimate look at the Grand Canyon.* TOM BEAN

skyline are the San Francisco Peaks. Franciscan missionaries saw the profile of these beautiful mountains from the Hopi mesas in 1629 and named them for their St. Francis. Mount Humphreys, at 12,633 feet, is the highest of four main peaks, and the highest in Arizona as well.

This is Coconino National Forest land, and any side road will take you higher into the ponderosa forest, through lovely aspen groves, and into towering spruce and fir.

In winter, the Peaks are a prime destination for downhill skiers and snowboarders. Seven miles from Flagstaff is the turnoff from U.S. 180 for the Arizona Snowbowl. Four chairlifts provide access to 30-some trails that can receive up to 260 inches of nice dry powder in a winter. The runs range from bunny slope to highly advanced. With a ski school and two lodges, the Snowbowl beckons to the laid-back skier and weekend lowlander.

Back at the Grand Canyon, once you've filled your senses with vistas, head out the East Rim Drive, past Desert View and the famous Watchtower, and out of the park. The road drops down off the East Kaibab Monocline, paralleling the awesome steep gorge carved by the Little Colorado River on its way to the main Colorado in Grand Canyon. Along the roadside, Navajo bead sellers work late at their stands.

At the junction of U.S. 89, turn north (left) and go

(BELOW) *A mile below Moran Point on the South Rim, the Colorado River seems tame.* JACK DYKINGA
(FAR LEFT) *Two skiers descend the south side of the Peaks at the Arizona Snowbowl.* MARC MUENCH
(LEFT) *Grand Falls on the Little Colorado River lies southeast of Wupatki National Monument.* STEWART AITCHISON

one mile to the Cameron Trading Post, perched on the edge of the Little Colorado River. I often stop here to partake of a Navajo taco. This is a golden brown circle of frybread, heaped with pinto beans, green chiles, lettuce, and cheese, barely contained by the plate. Foreign visitors stare at what the waitress has set before me, and with exuberant sign language I urge them to try one.

Cameron has been a crossroads of civilization in northern Arizona for at least eight decades. Its location, overlooking the Little Colorado along Jacob Hamblin's Mormon Trail, determined much of that significance. In 1916, brothers Hubert and C.D. Richardson built a trading post here, one of several posts run by the Richardson family across the western Navajo Reservation.

As with all reservation trading posts, Cameron served as headquarters for a system of symbiotic exchange: Wagon loads of sheep wool and piñon nuts brought in by Gray Mountain Navajos, who bartered for cloth, tobacco, and canned goods.

From the original wooden store and one-room cabins, the Cameron Trading Post has expanded and remodeled into a modern business that includes a motel, gift shop, gas station, post office, restaurant, and gallery. A Navajo weaver can often be found at work on her loom in the gift shop. The gardens behind the gallery are a wonderful refuge; there's a picnic table made of a single slab of sandstone that has to be seen to be believed.

Continuing south from Cameron, you arrive at the turnoff into Wupatki National Monument, the park's north entrance. The 36-mile loop road takes you through both Wupatki and Sunset Crater, and rejoins U.S. 89.

At Wupatki, the land is covered with platinum-colored grasses, punctuated with dark junipers and black-capped mesas. The eye-stretching view extends out across the valley of the Little Colorado and back towards the San Francisco Peaks. It is a silent land, except for the wind, which bends the flexible grass stalks and hinders the flight of the ravens.

The first stop in Wupatki is Lomaki and Box Canyon ruins. These two small pueblos flank the mouth of Box Canyon. Standing off by itself is Lomaki, which in the Hopi language means "beautiful house." It sits on the edge of an earth crack, a deep, narrow fissure in the bedrock limestone. Careful observation reveals crumbling walls atop many of the surrounding hills, signs of the bustling community that existed here back in the A.D. 1100s. In fact, within the park's 35,000 acres, nearly 2,700 sites have been documented — from pit houses, to pueblos, to rock art panels — evidencing a great mixing of cultures through time.

Not far from Lomaki, the Citadel stands atop a high hill. When Sunset Crater was an erupting volcano between 1065 and 1220, residents here would have enjoyed an amazing view of the pyrotechnical display. Terraced farmlands around the 30-room Citadel indicate people may have been taking advantage of the mulching effect of the cinders from the volcano or the increased rainfall during those years. At the base of the Citadel is Nalakihu Ruin, its 10 rooms burned and never reinhabited.

Traveling on through Antelope Prairie, I watch for antelope — more correctly pronghorn — speeding across the open grassland, the swiftest four-footed animals in

THE GRAND CANYON BY RAIL

Today, a round-trip ticket on the Grand Canyon Railway costs a little more than the $3.95 charged in September, 1901, when the train first chugged out of Williams, Arizona, for the South Rim of the Grand Canyon.

From 1901 until 1968, the Grand Canyon Railway carried passengers to the log depot in the famed national park, and let them off near historic El Tovar Hotel, where they could eat an elegant lunch, sightsee, and then return to Williams. Today, that same experience is once again possible.

While waiting to board at the 1908 Williams Depot, you can sip a cappuccino, view the museum, and enjoy the hilarity of the Cataract Creek Boys, one of several Old-West style live acts. Once aboard, the entertainment continues with exceedingly convincing "robbers" demanding your wallet and all your jewelry.

Since passenger service was restored in 1989, some 130,000 people a year now relive history on the train. In summer, vintage steam engines pull restored Pullman cars through grassland and forest at a leisurely pace. It takes about three hours to cover the 65 miles to the South Rim. In winter, diesel locomotives are employed. ▪

Just as in 1901, a steam engine of the Grand Canyon Railway brings passengers to the Grand Canyon. LES MANEVITZ

North America. This is where prehistoric people found the best soils for farming, where they placed their terraced fields, marked boundaries and created windbreaks with rows of stones, and built field houses where they kept rodents away from the stockpiled corn.

Traveling on, I arrive at the visitors center and, behind it, the namesake Wupatki Pueblo itself. The magnificent multistoried dwelling, with more than 100 rooms, is the largest site in the park. Though it no longer flows, a spring here was the reason for Wupatki's location during prehistoric times. A self-guiding tour leads through the pueblo and the adjacent amphitheater and ballcourt, an unusual feature for a northern Arizona site.

A short distance off the main road is another site, to my eyes the most breathtaking in the entire park. It is called Wukoki, and every time I see it, I'm awestruck. I simply stand at a distance and gaze upon it,

(LEFT) *Lomaki — the name means beautiful house — is one of the stops on the loop drive through Wupatki National Monument.* RICHARD MAACK
(RIGHT) *The 30-room Citadel Ruin rests on a high hill at Wupatki. Petroglyphs are visible on some of the rocks in foreground.* PATRICK FISCHER

rising seamlessly from a bedrock prominence, elegant and spare, its graceful lines speaking of the well-honed aesthetic sense of its builders. Wukoki still stands three stories high, the corners perfect, the stone slabs shaped with care, the masonry well executed. In the low light of late afternoon sun, the warm red walls fairly glow.

The contrast between Wupatki and neighboring Sunset Crater volcano could hardly be more striking. Sunset Crater is a moonscape of black cinders and twisted lava flows, looking so fresh they might have been deposited only a day or two ago. Many cinder cones rise above the plain, until the road finally passes right by the steep slopes of Sunset Crater. Although the 1,000-foot-high crater itself can no longer be climbed, the Lava Flow Trail at its base is a fine introduction to the byproducts of this, the youngest of 500 or so volcanoes in northern Arizona.

(BELOW) *The multistoried Wupatki, with more than 100 rooms, is the largest of the dwellings at Wupatki National Monument north of Flagstaff.* RANDY PRENTICE
(RIGHT) *Flowers thrive in the fields around Sunset Crater, which erupted more than 900 years ago.* ED TOLIVER

Best dates now have Sunset Crater first erupting in 1065 and continuing to spew gases, cinders, molten lava, and bombs for 200 years after. The mile-long Lava Flow Trail winds through the jumbled, treacherous terrain, past fascinating volcanic landforms such as clinkers, hornitos, spatter cones, and squeeze-ups. Dwarfed aspens and ponderosa pines struggle to grow on the rocky ground.

After a stop at the informative park visitors center, rejoin U.S. 89 and turn south to Flagstaff. ☘

When You Go

Arizona Snowbowl: North of Flagstaff. (520) 779-1951. For snow reports, call (602) 957-0404 in the Phoenix area; outside Phoenix, (520) 779-4577.

Coconino National Forest: Supervisor's Office, 2323 E. Greenlaw Lane, Flagstaff. (520) 527-3600.

Grand Canyon National Park/South Rim: P.O. Box 129, Grand Canyon, AZ 86023. (520) 638-7888. Admission fee. The park visitors center is a good first stop to help you plan your visit. A short distance away, the Yavapai Museum will provide more information about how the Canyon came to be. Web sites: www.nps.gov/grca/ or www.thecanyon.com/nps/

South Rim campgrounds: Mather Campground, reservations required March 1 through Nov. 30, call (800) 365-2267. At other times and at Desert View Campground, sites available on a first-come basis. For online camping reservations, go to Web site: reservations.nps.gov/

South Rim RV camping: A facility with 84 sites and hookups, showers, and laundry facilities is located near Mather Campground. For reservations, call (800) 365-2267.

South Rim lodging: There are six lodges within the park on the South Rim, one just outside the South Rim entrance, and Phantom Ranch at the bottom of the Canyon. Together they provide about 1,000 rooms and cabins. For reservations, (up to 23 months in advance), call (303) 29PARKS or (520) 638-2631.

Grand Canyon Railway: 1201 W. Route 66, Ste. 200, Flagstaff. Reservations, (800) 843-8724. Web site: www.thetrain.com

Kaibab National Forest: Supervisor's Office, Williams, (520) 635-8200. Chalender Ranger District, Williams, (520) 635-2676. Tusayan Ranger District, Tusayan, (520) 638-2443.

Sunset Crater Volcano and Wupatki national monuments: Off State 89, Flagstaff. (520) 526-0502 and 679-2365. Admission fee.

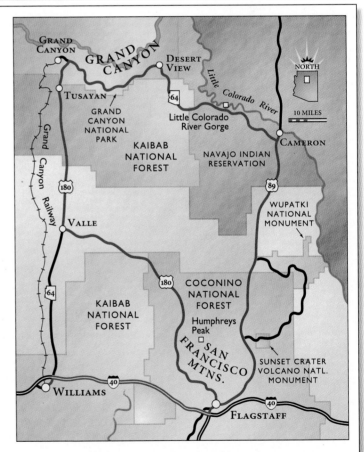

Summer camping at U.S. Forest Service's Bonito Campground by Sunset Crater entrance. Web sites: www.nps.gov/sucr/ and www.nps.gov/wupa/

Williams-Grand Canyon Chamber of Commerce: 200 W. Railroad Avenue, Williams. (520) 635-4061 or (800) 863-0546.

High Desert Navajo and Hopi Country

ANCIENT SITES, GEOLOGIC WONDERS

by Rose Houk

As I stood looking out at the magnificent cliff dwelling called Betatakin, a flock of turkey vultures gathered and circled over the canyon. A rough count revealed nearly 30 of the large birds, coming together, I speculated, for their annual autumn migration. Could such a gathering have been a signal to the people who once lived here that it was also time for them to migrate? It had been another severely dry summer, their granaries were empty, and they faced the prospect of a bitter cold winter they weren't sure they could survive.

For those who lived here 700 years ago, moving was probably nothing new. The Hopi Indians, who today live 50 miles to the south, speak of migrations made by various clans. Often, they say, a sign appeared, telling them it was time to go. Some Hopi clans consider Betatakin a sacred ancestral home. They call the place *Kawestima*, or North Village, and the people who lived there, the *Hisatsinom*, "the long ago people." Archaeologists refer to them as the Anasazi.

Betatakin, now preserved in Navajo National Monument in northeast Arizona, was not a home for very long. Though great effort was expended to construct the 135-room pueblo under the cliff's sweeping alcove, the Anasazi lived here fewer than 50 years, from about A.D.1250 to 1300. Why would they put forth so much labor only to walk away after such a short time? Archaeologists look to long-lasting drought, social problems, disease, or a combination of such causes to explain the departure.

Staring down at the silent stone rooms and beyond to the wild fastness of the Tsegi Canyon system, I wondered if the Anasazi might have come here for the spectacular scenery: labyrinths of canyons, twisting and turning; walls of slickrock colored peach and salmon; and high plateau country dashed with dark piñon pine and juniper trees, soft fringed sagebrush, dusty-leafed buffaloberry, and fragrant-flowered fendlerbush.

It was to all these useful plants (and animals too) that the people owed their lives and visions.

Towns & sites: Page, Kaibito Plateau, Navajo National Monument, Kayenta, Monument Valley, Chinle, Canyon de Chelly, Ganado, Hubbell Trading Post, Hopi mesas, and Tuba City.

Overview: In northeastern Arizona, you'll roam over plateaus, alongside and over canyons, and over high desert country and mesas where prehistoric pueblos tell the story of ancient ones and stone monoliths rise from the desert floor.

Routes & mileage: Starting in Page, this trip will cover nearly 500 miles, including tours at sites along the way. Take State Route 98 for 66 miles to its junction with U.S. Route 160. Turn east (left) and go 12 miles to State 564, the turnoff to Navajo National Monument. It is another nine miles to the monument. Return to U.S. 160, go east (left) 20 miles to Kayenta. Turn north onto U.S. 163, and drive 22 miles to Monument Valley. From Monument Valley, return to Kayenta, take U.S. 160 for eight miles east, then turn south on Navajo Route 59 and a 58-mile drive to Many Farms. Turn south (right) onto U.S. 191 and drive 15 miles on Navajo Route 64, turn east and in a few miles you'll be at Chinle and Canyon de Chelly. After touring Canyon de Chelly, return to U.S. 191 for a 30-mile drive south to the intersection with State 264, turn east (right) to Ganado and Hubbell Trading Post. From Ganado, go west for about 62 miles on State 264 to Second Mesa on the Hopi Reservation. Continue west on State 264 for 62 miles to Tuba City. Take U.S. 160 west for 10 miles to U.S. 89. From there, you can go north to Page or south to Flagstaff.

Time to allow: Three days.

(LEFT) *The ruins of Betatakin, consisting of 135 rooms, lie in an alcove at the upper left.* DAVID MUENCH
(ABOVE, RIGHT) *Rock formations seem to erupt from the sand dunes of Monument Valley.* JACK DYKINGA
(RIGHT) *Visiting Keet Seel, a cliff dwelling of more than 150 rooms, requires a 17-mile round-trip hike from the monument's visitors center.* LAURENCE PARENT

And in this arid, rocky country, it was water that brought them here — water from seeps and springs dripping from the backs of alcoves and the heads of canyons, and in some places, even the miracle of a free-flowing stream.

To get here from Page, you travel southeast across the high shrub and grass desert of the Kaibito Plateau, with the great blue dome of Navajo Mountain ever present on the northern horizon, eastward through Marsh Pass with Black Mesa over your right shoulder, then north up onto the Shonto Plateau.

This is "Rez" country, home to Navajo, Hopi, and Paiute. It's big country, a landscape with an infinite horizon. It's subtle country, colored in pastel light, changing constantly as clouds come and go. It's intriguing country, filled with suggestions of people living lives out of the mainstream. The hand-lettered signs along the road are a clue: FAT SHEEP. HAY FOR SALE. SQUAW DANCE. REVIVAL TONITE.

A sandy track leads to a small round dwelling, like an overturned mud bowl. It's a traditional Navajo hogan. Nearby, long juniper poles are stacked upright, firewood for the winter. Most Navajo homesteads include a separate house or trailer as a summer shade house and almost always have a wooden corral. Out on a flat spot is a field of bushy corn, with a scarecrow flapping wildly at marauding birds.

The Navajo National Monument is a tiny parcel of federal land amid the Navajo Nation. The visitors center's small museum displays the arts and crafts of the prehistoric people of the Kayenta region: their exquisite pottery, yucca sandals, and stone and wood tools. You can also step into a replica of a typical masonry room, with a row of mealing bins and a granary for storing food.

From the visitors center, the Sandal Trail, a paved path along the rim, leads to the overlook of Betatakin. Nearby, the Aspen Forest Overlook Trail, less than a mile round trip, drops down into the head of the canyon where Betatakin is located. Though Betatakin isn't in sight, you can see the reason for its location. A spring feeds lush growth of Douglas fir, water birch, white-barked aspens, and twisted Gambel oak.

The campground here is one of the quietest and most pleasant in any of the national parks. Spend the night and be first in line at the visitors center in the morning to go with a ranger on the walk down into Betatakin. If you have even more time, and have made a reservation, you can hike to Keet Seel, one of the largest pueblo sites in Arizona. It is a 17-mile round trip, allowed only from Memorial Day through Labor Day.

From Navajo National Monument, head east on U.S. 160 into the town of Kayenta, gas up, and continue north on U.S. 163 to Monument Valley Tribal Park on the Utah border. The famous "monuments" of isolated standing

(ABOVE) *Two Navajo shepherds tend sheep at Sand Springs Wash in Monument Valley.* JAMES TALLON

(RIGHT) *Rising from the desert floor, the rock formations of Monument Valley seem to change as clouds waft over and the sun travels its course over them.* RANDY PRENTICE

rock have become icons of the American West. People from all over the world come to marvel at them. On any day at Monument Valley, the parking lot is a polyglot scene of German, French, Australian, Japanese, and English visitors jockeying for tours in open-air trucks with Navajo guides.

With a guide, you can enter the backcountry and see the more private, hidden parts of the valley and the hogans of Navajo residents who still ride horses and graze sheep and whose hands, gnarled as yucca root, still weave intricate wool rugs. On the backroad tour, you will also see elegant rock arches like Eye of the Sun.

Horse rides and hikes of varying lengths are also available with guides. A self-guided tour on the unpaved 17-mile road is another way to see Monument Valley. The road, mostly one-way, is usually passable to regular passenger vehicles, unless rains have been especially heavy. The posted speed limit is five miles per hour, so allow at least a couple of hours for the drive.

The shapes of some of the rock formations have inspired their names: Mittens, Totem Pole, Three Sisters. Others, like Mitchell Mesa and Merrick Butte, commemorate early prospectors who ran into trouble in Monument Valley. The Navajo, or Diné, call all of Monument Valley *Tse' Bii' Ndzisgaii*, "space between the rocks." But when I asked Navajo guide Omar Ateen if his people had names for each monument, he said they were sacred and could be spoken only by the medicine men when they came here. To them, the individual buttes and spires hold water and support the sky. They are the holy beings.

Though Monument Valley's formations appear immutable, in a geologic sense they are temporary. Eroded

from once-solid and continuous masses of rock, they are still being formed today. The soft sand dunes throughout the valley are simply the finest pieces of the rock, waiting to be washed and blown away. The formations seem to change hour by hour, as early morning clouds hover on the tops and waft away like smoke, and as the sun reflects off their faceted faces.

After your Monument Valley adventure, it's time for some rest at Goulding's Lodge and Trading Post, on the west side of U.S. 163 tucked up against Big Rock Door Mesa. This establishment's founder, Harry Goulding, lured film director John Ford here. Starting in 1938 with John Wayne starring in *Stagecoach*, Ford made a number of films with Monument Valley as the backdrop. Along with the motel, dining room, gift shop, and campground, Goulding's maintains the trading post as a museum filled with Monument Valley memorabilia. Outside the post is a brush ramada. At sunrise, there is no better place to watch the soft pink light slip over Monument Valley.

From Monument Valley, head back to Kayenta and on to Canyon de Chelly National Monument. Within the park is the namesake Canyon de Chelly (pronounced da-shay), a stunning defile of copper sandstone lined with green cottonwoods. Joining Canyon de Chelly from the north is Canyon del Muerto. For at least 1,500 years, various groups of Native Americans have called this place home, from early pit house dwellers, to Ancestral Puebloans, to the present-day Navajo, for whom this is a place of great importance.

Take part of the day for the 21-mile drive along the south rim of Canyon de Chelly, where several stops offer stunning views into the canyon. From Junction Overlook, you can see two prehistoric cliff dwellings, First Ruin and Junction Ruin.

A few more miles along, White House Overlook affords a look at the famous White House Ruin, a large multistory masonry pueblo that dates to as early as A.D. 1060.

If you're feeling frisky, you can hike down the mile-and-a-half trail to White House Ruin. Though administered by the National Park Service, Canyon de Chelly is unique because it remains tribal land and home to the Navajo. White House Ruin is the only place you can go in the canyon without a Navajo guide. This hike is steep coming out, a consideration on a hot summer day, but it gives an excellent taste of the world inside Canyon de Chelly.

Travel by foot in and out of the canyon has long been a regular routine for residents of Canyon de Chelly. Traditionally, they spent summers in the canyon and winters on the rim. Some still maintain that pattern. Don't be

surprised to see a Navajo grandmother, in full-tiered skirt and tennis shoes, hiking the trail in front of you.

Back on top, continue along the south rim to Spider Rock Overlook, where the canyon is 1,000 feet deep. The Navajo say 800-foot-high Spider Rock is the home of Spider Woman, who taught them how to weave.

Thunderbird Lodge is a lovely place to spend the night at Canyon de Chelly. At the turn of the century a trading post was built on this site, which later became "Cozy" McSparron's Thunderbird Ranch. The Thunderbird serves as headquarters for trips up the canyon in nearly indestructible six-wheeled vehicles the Navajo guides jokingly call "Shake and Bakes."

On a rainy September day, I and a large group of French visitors all hopped in the back of one of these trucks. We lumbered up the shallow wash that was flowing with mocha-colored water. Every time the truck dipped into the soft, sandy streambed, my fellow travelers exclaimed in unison, "Oooh la la!" Our guide, David Bia, was born and raised in Canyon del Muerto. As we headed up del Muerto, David pointed out handprints and other figures painted in white on the sandstone wall. They were made by the Anasazi, the Navajo word for the prehistoric dwellers. He defined "Anasazi" as "those who have drifted, or passed, on," while others say a close translation is "enemy ancestors." Navajo hunting scenes and Hopi clan signs were also pecked onto the natural canvas. For a time, explained David, the Hopi and Navajo lived here together peacefully. Tucked on streamside terraces were the summer camps of present Navajo residents, where they tend fields of corn, squash, watermelon, beans, alfalfa, and fruit trees. One family passed by in a pickup truck, its bed loaded with freshly harvested corn.

Farther up del Muerto, we were treated to views of Antelope House and Standing Cow Ruin, where a large white cow has been painted on the canyon wall. It is an important symbol, related to the Long Walk, an event central to Navajo history. In 1864, the U.S. Army drove thousands of Navajo out of Canyon de Chelly and other parts of their homeland. The Navajo were marched to Fort Sumner, or Bosque Redondo, in New Mexico, and held for four years. After returning to Canyon de Chelly, they were given livestock, and it is this return of their animals that the Standing Cow represents.

About 35 miles south of Canyon de Chelly via U.S. 191 and State 264 is the town of Ganado. Presbyterian missionaries arrived here at the turn of the 20th century, eventually building a school, church, and health facilities on a campus that is now home to the Navajo Health Foundation and Sage Memorial Hospital. Services are still held in the lovely stone church, built in 1941, and in the homey dining hall called Cafe Sage, you can get an inexpensive breakfast or lunch.

A half mile west, across a wooden bridge under large spreading cottonwoods, sits Hubbell Trading Post. Now a national historic site, it is one of the oldest continuously operating trading posts in the Navajo Nation. In 1878, at age 23, John Lorenzo Hubbell started his career here as trader to the Navajo. In 1902, he and his wife, Lina Rubi, moved into the thick-walled, low-slung adobe house beside the post. Hubbell became known to the Navajo as "Double Glasses" and "Old Mexican."

Besides trading coffee, cloth, and canned fruit for sheep wool and piñon nuts, Hubbell was known for his hospitality to outside travelers, among them President Theodore Roosevelt.

"He always had his door open," said the park ranger who guided us through the Hubbell home.

With his wife and their four children, Hubbell spent 50 years at this self-sustaining homestead with its own bread oven behind the house, a crowing rooster in the barnyard, and a garden full of corn and vegetables. Hubbell and his sons eventually built up an empire of nearly 30 posts and other businesses throughout the Southwest. After Hubbell's death in 1930, his sons carried on, and his daughter Dorothy lived at the homestead until 1967, when it officially became National Park Service property. John Lorenzo Hubbell is buried in the family cemetery on the hill overlooking the home.

Modern-day trader Bill Malone continues to buy and sell beautiful Navajo weavings, stacked several feet high in the cedar-scented rug room of the post. You can find Crystal, Wide Ruins, and Storm patterns, everything from small tabletop weavings priced around $200 to large, old chief blankets carrying an $18,000 tag.

Hubbell Trading Post is recent history compared to

(LEFT) *Hopi artist Ronald Honyoati created this kachina depicting a harvest of prickly pear cactus.* COURTESY GALLERY 10, SCOTTSDALE. (BELOW) *Samples of Hopi pottery — clockwise from top left: wedding vase by Joy Navasie, tall vase by Gloria Kahe (a Navajo potter doing Hopi styles), large jar by Mark Tahbo, jar by Tonita Nampeyo, jar by Iris Youvella, and bowl by Rondina Huma.* COURTESY KEAMS CANYON ARTS AND CRAFTS. BOTH BY JERRY JACKA (RIGHT) *Sandstone spires and sheer cliffs weave a maze in Coal Mine Canyon on the Navajo Reservation.* TOM DANIELSEN

what you'll find on the Hopi Reservation. The Hopi have lived on the three high mesas in northern Arizona for at least a thousand years. There are 12 villages, one of which, Old Oraibi, dating at least to A.D. 1150, is said to be the oldest still-inhabited town in North America.

From every village, the Hopi have a constant view of *Nuvatukya'ovi*, the San Francisco Peaks. From July until the winter solstice, the spiritual beings called *katsinas* (kachinas) reside on the Peaks, returning to the mesas the rest of the year in an annual cycle that has everything to do with bringing prosperity, rain, and fertility to the Hopi.

The Hopi are warm and hospitable, but they carefully guard their religious ceremonies and ritual knowledge. At times, visitors have shown disrespect or taken advantage of their good nature. Consequently, visitors must have permission to be in any village and must not take photographs or make drawings or recordings. Some social dances are open to non-Hopi, but inquire first at the Hopi Cultural Center on Second Mesa. The cultural center, with lodge, restaurant, and small museum, is a good first stop where you can fortify yourself with traditional hominy stew or a Hopi burger on blue corn frybread.

The Hopi are renowned for making fine crafts — silver jewelry, baskets, pottery, and kachina carvings — which can be purchased at many galleries and shops along the main highway. Tsakurshovi, 1.5 miles east of the cultural center, is a small shop owned by Janice and Joseph Day. Smoldering sweetgrass scents the air, gourds fill cardboard boxes, and fine pots and interesting kachina carvings are on display. One of the Days' most famous items is the T-shirt bearing the slogan: "Don't Worry — Be Hopi." As Janice explained, it goes back to her father, a farmer, who worried when there was either too little or too much rain for his corn. The only logical response, she laughed, was the saying on the T-shirt.

Continuing northwest on State 264, you come to Coal Mine Canyon, which offers a stunning view of elaborate rock formations. On your right about 16 miles from Tuba City, take a dirt road across a cattle guard to a windmill about a quarter mile off the highway. There, you'll find a picnic area and a canyon overview.

At State 264's intersection with U.S. 160 is the Tuba City Truck Stop: Don't pass up the Navajo tacos here. If it's Saturday, you may want to visit the roadside flea market, where you can obtain everything from popcorn balls, tools, and clothing, to herbs like mountain tobacco. In uptown Tuba City, the octagonal stone Tuba City Trading Post, established in 1870, still operates. It was bought by the Babbitt brothers in 1905 and restored in the 1980s.

From Tuba City, take U.S. 160 west for 10 miles to U.S. 89. From there, you can go north to Page or south to Flagstaff. ◪

When You Go

NOTE: In Arizona, only the Navajo Nation observes daylight saving time (Mountain) from April through October. That is one hour ahead of the rest of Arizona, including the Hopi Reservation.

When visiting Navajo and Hopi lands, practice the same etiquette as you would when visiting someone's home. Do not trespass or invade people's privacy. Photographs of individuals may be taken only with their permission. When driving, be aware of livestock on the roads and of low areas prone to flash flooding. Get permits before driving on unpaved backroads.

Navajo Nation: Window Rock. The Navajo Nation administers all government services, permits, and traffic enforcement. Navajo Nation Tourism Department, (520) 871-6436. Ask whether your plans need a backcountry permit. Navajo Parks and Recreation Department, (520) 871-6647.

Navajo National Monument: (520) 672-2367. No entrance fee. Visitors center open all year. Betatakin guided hikes usually run May through September. The steep trail is five miles round trip. The campground is open year-round on a first-come, first-served basis. For the strenuous 8.5-mile hike to Keet Seel and overnight stay, call months in advance for details and reservations (only 20 people per day). Web site: www.nps.gov/nava

Monument Valley Tribal Park: Monument Valley, Utah. (435) 727-3353. Entrance fee. Visitors center, campground.

Goulding's Lodge: Monument Valley, Utah. (435) 727-3231. Lodge, museum, campground, gas, groceries. Web site: www.navajotribalpark.com

Canyon de Chelly National Monument: Chinle. (520) 674-5500. Hiking or driving in the canyon requires fee, permit, and authorized Navajo guide. Web site: www.nps.gov/cach

Thunderbird Lodge: Chinle. (800) 679-2437 or (520) 674-5841. Call for reservations for lodging, jeep tours into the canyon, or guided hikes and horseback rides.

Hubbell Trading Post National Historic Site: Ganado. (520) 755-3475. Day-use area only. Web site: www.nps.gov/hutr

Hopi Cultural Center: Second Mesa. (520) 734-2401. Restaurant, motel, small museum (with entrance fee). Web site: www.hopionline.com

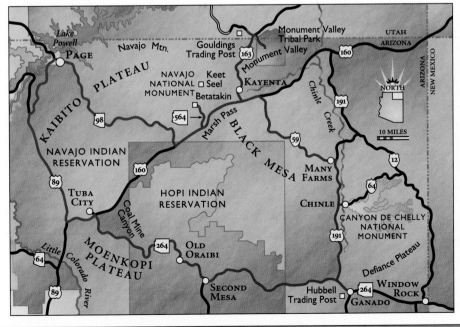

Lake Powell, North Rim, Pipe Spring

by Rose Houk

Time was running out for Fathers Dominguez and Escalante. A cold winter was bearing down on the two Franciscan friars as they worked their way across what is now the Arizona Strip. With their food supply exhausted, they were reduced to eating their horses and the fat brown pine nuts given to them by Indians.

It was October, 1776, and the priests and their fellow explorers had been on a momentous expedition for two months. They had departed from Santa Fe, then under Spain's rule, and were bound for Monterey, California. In western Utah, they faced the unwelcome realization that delays, hardships, and weather conspired to prevent them from reaching their destination.

Turning back south and then east, Dominguez and Escalante had by mid-October reached the Vermilion Cliffs and Paria Plateau in northern Arizona and were searching futilely for a suitable place to cross the Colorado River. Zigzagging to avoid topographical obstacles, they took 10 days to reach a point on the river that is now Lees Ferry. Here, they found the river too deep and too wide to negotiate. As a sign of their desperation, they named their camp *Salsipuedes*, "get out if you can."

It was November now, and scouts had gone ahead to locate a ford. At last, they descended Padre Creek on the north side of the Colorado and sent out the best swimmers to test the waters. It was more than satisfactory, and every man and horse made it safely across. On the far side, the party fired muskets and sang praises to the Lord.

This historic place, called the Crossing of the Fathers, now lies deep under the waters of Lake Powell.

"Captain Betty" pointed out the site as we cruised Lake Powell's Padre Bay in a 61-foot, double-deck tour boat named *Lady Grace*. We were on our way to Rainbow Bridge National Monument, where a magnificent sandstone arch spans Bridge Canyon and frames Navajo Mountain.

Sipping coffee and chatting with Betty as she kept a close eye on the other boats roaring by, I stared at the

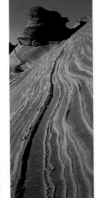

Towns & sites: Page, Lake Powell, Glen Canyon Dam, Marble Canyon, Lees Ferry, Jacob Lake, Kaibab National Forest, North Rim of the Grand Canyon, Fredonia, and Pipe Spring National Monument.

Overview: Before starting the drive to the North Rim, you can tour Glen Canyon Dam, Carl Hayden Visitors Center, Lake Powell, and the Glen Canyon National Recreation Area. Lake Powell is one of the country's largest artificial lakes, with many recreational opportunities. On the rest of the tour, you'll see historic ferry and settlement sites on the Colorado River, the Arizona Strip, low desert and high plateau scenery, and the North Rim of the Grand Canyon.

Routes & mileage: About 350 miles total. From Page, take U.S. Route 89 south for 25 miles to U.S. 89A. From there, it's about 15 miles to Marble Canyon. Leave U.S. 89A at Marble Canyon for a five-mile trip to Lees Ferry. Back at Marble Canyon, continue on U.S. 89A for 41 miles to Jacob Lake; State Route 67 for 45 miles to the North Rim; back to Jacob Lake; west on 89A for 30 miles to Fredonia; west on State Route 389 for 15 miles to Pipe Spring National Monument. From there, it's 125 miles to Page via 389, 89A, and 89. Or, you can take 89A at Fredonia for seven miles to U.S. 89 and then east for 85 miles to Page.

Time to allow: Three or four days.

(LEFT) *Lake Powell's shoreline takes in canyon after canyon — this one is Gunsight Canyon.* GARY LADD
(ABOVE, RIGHT) *Red and yellow bands distinguish petrified sand dunes in the Paria Canyon-Vermilion Cliffs Wilderness near Lees Ferry.* JACK DYKINGA
(RIGHT) *A sandstone arch lies in the midst of Lake Powell at Rainbow Bridge National Monument.* JERRY SEIVE

crossing site and tried to imagine what Dominguez and Escalante endured — living on nuts and berries and the flesh of their horses, making a map of the country as they went, traveling under their own power and by their own wits. Today, travelers through this country worry mostly about finding a telephone that works, a gas station that's open, and a good hamburger along the way. Indeed, times have changed.

What may have changed the most is the landscape. The towering sandstone mesas and deep narrow canyons are still glorious to behold. But we see only a portion of them, for they are inundated by the turquoise waters of Lake Powell. This was once the free-flowing Colorado River, which carved Glen Canyon. Extending upstream for 186 miles, Lake Powell is the nation's second-largest artificial lake (Lake Mead downstream near Las Vegas is the largest). As Betty told us, there are 96 major canyons on Lake Powell and a shoreline of nearly 2,000 miles, more than the entire West Coast. All told, the Glen Canyon National Recreation Area encompasses nearly a million acres.

Three million people come here every year to play, most of them launching houseboats and powerboats at one of the five marinas on the lake. Wahweap, where the *Lady Grace* and other tour boats are docked, is the main marina, closest to the town of Page. Houseboats tow smaller boats and all manner of "personal watercraft" with which houseboaters can explore the scores of skinny side canyons. Anglers venture onto Lake Powell to try their luck at catching the prized striped bass. Hikers

(ABOVE) *From Lake Powell's Padre Bay, Navajo Mountain looms on the horizon at left. The rock (left-center) overlooking the water is Gunsight Butte.* GEORGE H.H. HUEY (BELOW) *Fishing is excellent in the cold, clear water of the Colorado River below Glen Canyon Dam.* RICHARD MAACK (RIGHT) *A wall of Marble Canyon is reflected in the Colorado River near Lees Ferry.* DAVID MUENCH

find endless slickrock country in every direction from the lake.

To see the inner workings of Glen Canyon Dam, which created Lake Powell, you can take a self-guided tour from the Carl Hayden visitors center on the outskirts of Page. With brochure in hand, I rode down the elevator 110 feet

with fluorescent tubes. A sign reassured me that there was 100 feet of concrete between me and Lake Powell.

The hall led into the power plant, where eight huge, yellow generators hummed as the water of the Colorado River turned turbine blades and whirling rotors. Those generators convert water power into electricity, enough for a million people and enough to earn $140 million dollars a year in hydroelectric power sales.

With all that to ponder, I headed out of Page on U.S. 89 south to Marble Canyon and Lees Ferry, to stick my toes into the dancing waters of the Colorado River, fresh and cold from the depths of Lake Powell. Adventurers were rigging their rafts at the ramp at Lees Ferry, the launch spot for Grand Canyon trips. Some friends were helping them find space on the tiny rubber rafts for two weeks' supply of beer.

Lees Ferry is one of those special places in the West, a confluence of history and geography. The Echo Cliffs and Vermilion Cliffs meet here. The Paria River joins the Colorado River. Though it didn't work for Fathers Dominguez and Escalante, this location has long served as one of the few crossing points for hundreds of miles along the Colorado. With the aid of a ferry, it was a key link for Mormon colonists traveling from Utah to Arizona.

John D. Lee started the ferry and a ranch here in 1871. Emma Lee, one of his many wives, lived on the ranch and ran the ferry. She called the place Lonely Dell. I always like to visit Lonely Dell, strolling through the orchard with the old stone-lined irrigation ditches, stopping by Emma's cabin to wonder what she might have

to the crest of the dam. Over my right shoulder, I looked down the sweeping concrete face of the dam, 700 feet below to the swirling, green waters of the Colorado. Over my left shoulder, in much closer view, stretched the still, blue waters of the lake. Down 700 feet in another elevator, ears popping, I stepped out into a chilly, tiled hallway lit

said as she sat on the porch after a long day of work, watching the colors change on the high cliffs.

Down by the launch ramp, a mile-long trail along the riverbank leads to an old rock fort and post office, to the boiler and other equipment left from Charles Spencer's gold dredging operations, and to the original ferry crossing site, where Emma and her sons ran out to shuttle travelers across the great, untamed Colorado.

At Marble Canyon Lodge on U.S. 89, I grabbed a bite to eat and stopped in at the nearby Navajo Bridge Interpretive Center. The center was built along with the new, wider bridge that was finished in 1995. Fortunately, the old bridge was saved, and pedestrians can walk out on it and take a gander down at the swirling river.

I continued driving west, along the base of the Vermilion Cliffs, through high, wide, and lonesome House Rock Valley, still following in the tracks of Fathers Dominguez and Escalante. As I drove, I kept my eyes peeled for shadows cast by a particular, very large bird. California condors have been reintroduced into the wild here, the only place besides California where they live outside captivity. With a nine-foot wingspan, California condors are among the largest raptors in the world. They are also among the most endangered. The Vermilion Cliffs provide an ideal habitat for them, and biologists track their movements and provide them with calf carcasses to eat. A few of the condors have traveled 100 miles in a day.

Before me, the great swell of the Kaibab Plateau rose from the valley floor. Twisting and winding, the road climbed up the eastern flank of the plateau, nearly 3,000 feet from the valley to the top. I tried to time my arrival for a chocolate milk shake at Jacob Lake Inn and for a stop at the Kaibab Plateau visitors center next door to check out the interesting exhibits and well-stocked book and map store.

From Jacob Lake, the drive to the North Rim of the Grand Canyon is surely one of the most scenic in the West. At this elevation, between 7,000 and 8,000 feet, you pass through a fairyland forest of ponderosa pine, fir, spruce, and aspen. In mid- to late September, the aspen gleam golden among the dark evergreens. Large grassy meadows, called "parks," create expansive breaks in the walls of trees and in summer are dappled with wildflowers. Mule deer are often out grazing in the meadows. Deer have always been abundant on the Kaibab and earned it another name, Buckskin Mountain.

The Grand Canyon, as always, is a wondrous surprise. The view from the North Rim is even more astounding because here the Canyon's dimension and depth is greater than on the south. It is a more complex scene of intricately carved buttes and spires, marching rank upon rank into the distance.

(ABOVE) *Sunrise sets the Vermilion Cliffs ablaze as the Colorado River sweeps around the Paria River delta toward Marble Canyon.* GARY LADD (LEFT) *This panorama takes in cliffs in the Saddle Mountain Wilderness, Marble Canyon, and Navajo Mountain.* ROBERT McDONALD (RIGHT) *On the North Rim, Cape Royal ranks among the most popular places to peer down into the seemingly endless rock tiers of the Grand Canyon.* GEORGE STOCKING

Occasionally, fog sweeps in and out of the Canyon, teasing the tips of the spires, something so ephemeral against something so ageless.

From the lodge on the Rim, you can take a short walk out to Bright Angel Point for a fine spectacle of the mile-deep Canyon. The more intimate Transept Trail leaves from the lodge and passes through the forest along the edge of Transept Canyon, which anywhere else would win national park status but here is only a small side canyon of the mother canyon. More committed hikers can start down into the canyon on the North Kaibab Trail. Roads lead out to Point Imperial and to Cape Royal on the Walhalla Plateau. A stop at peaceful Greenland Lake will often reward a patient person with sightings of wild turkey, deer, or perhaps a blue grouse.

The North Rim is the quiet side of the Grand Canyon: A shorter season (usually mid-May to mid-October) means smaller crowds and less development. The greatest pressure here is to make sure you get a seat on the lodge's porch to revel in a canyon sunset.

From the Canyon, head back past Jacob Lake and

(OPPOSITE PAGE, TOP) *Hikers descend the North Kaibab Trail, which crosses the Colorado.* GEORGE McCULLOUGH (OPPOSITE PAGE, BOTTOM) *Mount Hayden stands distinctively in the Grand Canyon. Here, it is viewed at sunset from Point Imperial on the North Rim.* ROBERT BLUE (RIGHT) *Winsor Castle was built by Mormons as a fort in 1872 at Pipe Spring.* KERRICK JAMES

onto Fredonia and Pipe Spring National Monument. Along the way, you'll have spectacular views of the "Grand Staircase," a series of varicolored cliffs rising in stair step fashion into the wilds of southern Utah.

A parade of history has passed Pipe Spring. At the base of the Hurricane Cliffs a flowing spring has lured people here for millennia, Native Americans, Mormon missionaries, cowboys, and government surveyors among them. It was the Mormons who settled permanently at Pipe Spring. They began cattle ranching, and to protect their herds and the valuable water source, Anson Perry Winsor oversaw construction of a two-story stone fort over the spring itself. It was called Winsor Castle and was finished in 1872.

Saunter around the grounds to see the orchards and gardens, the blacksmith shop and harness room, and the small rock bunkhouse where John Wesley Powell's survey crew stayed. Through the heavy gates of the fort, you enter the courtyard, where newly married Mormon couples traveling the Honeymoon Trail stopped for dances. You can go inside the furnished rooms and big kitchen where people lived and took their meals when the fort was converted to a ranch house. You can also see the room that housed Arizona's first telegraph and the spring room, where cheese and milk were kept cool and where the faint sound of trickling water can still be heard. ◨

When You Go

Fredonia Chamber of Commerce: (520) 643-7241.

Glen Canyon National Recreation Area/Lake Powell: Page. (520) 608-6200 or 608-6404. Boat tours, boat rentals, lodging, and RV parks run by Lake Powell Resorts & Marinas, (800) 528-6154. Reservations highly advisable for the half- and full-day tours to Rainbow Bridge. To see what Glen Canyon was like before the dam, take a float trip down the 15 miles of river below the dam. Contact Wilderness River Outfitters, (520) 645-3279, for information.

Grand Canyon Lodge/North Rim: Central reservations for rooms and cabins, (303) 297-2757.

Grand Canyon National Park/North Rim: (520) 638-7888, including weather information. Admission fee. North Rim visitor facilities open May 15 until October 15. After mid-October, the North Rim remains open for day-use only, until heavy snows close the road into the park. Reservations for the 82-site campground available by calling (800) 365-2267. Web sites: *www.nps.gov/grca/* or *www.thecanyon.com/nps/*

Jacob Lake Inn: (520) 643-7232.

Kaibab National Forest: Kaibab Plateau visitors center, U.S. 89A/State 67, Jacob Lake, (520) 643-7298. Open summer months only. North Kaibab Ranger District, Fredonia, (520) 643-7395.

Marble Canyon Lodge: (520) 355-2225 or (800) 726-1789.

Page-Lake Powell Chamber of Commerce/Visitors Bureau: (520) 645-2741 or toll-free, (888) 261-7243.

Pipe Spring National Monument: (520) 643-7105. Admission fee.

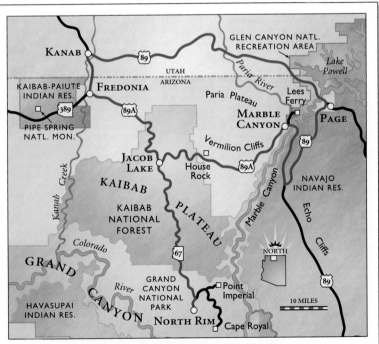

Natural Beauty and Small Town Charm

by Leo Banks

Any tour that begins in Payson must also begin with Zane Grey, the popular and prolific author who played such a role in making the area famous. From 1908 to 1939, he wrote 65 Western novels, many set in the canyons, draws, and glens around this picturesque community. With the possible exception of Tombstone and Wyatt Earp, no Arizona town is more closely associated with one man.

When he wasn't exploring the forests on horseback, a lap board balanced across his saddle for taking notes, Grey did much of his writing at a cabin 23 miles outside town. Built in 1920 and once a favorite of tourists, it burned to the ground in a 1990 forest fire.

But the next best thing, right on Main Street, is the Zane Grey Museum. Displays include some of the author's clothes and artifacts saved from the fire, movie posters, all of his books, and a video profile. Mel Counseller, a former caretaker at the Grey cabin, ran the museum until his death. Counseller knew intimate details of Grey's life and wasn't bad at spinning a story himself.

Some years back, when he was taking a group through the cabin, he struck up a conversation with a little fellow from California. Everyone else was giving the man sidelong glances and nudging their partners, as though he were some kind of celebrity.

"Say, what's your name?" Counseller asked.

"Dustin Hoffman," the little man replied.

Counseller didn't know he was talking to one of America's finest actors.

"What do you do, Dustin?" he asked.

Everyone in the room cracked up, especially Hoffman.

"I'd never seen one of his movies," Counseller said, chuckling when he recalled the encounter. "But he's read every one of Zane's books."

Another attraction, the Payson Candle Factory, with 5,500 square feet of space, is one of the largest candle shops in the country, featuring sculpted candles hand-carved by local craftsmen and a Christmas room open year-round.

Towns and sites: Payson, Tonto Natural Bridge State Park, Pine, Strawberry, Coconino National Forest, Winslow, Holbrook, Petrified Forest National Park, Heber, Sitgreaves National Forest, and Woods Canyon Recreation Area.

Overview: From the heavenly green of a ponderosa pine forest to the moonscape of the Painted Desert, this tour offers a wide variety of natural beauty, with a touch of small-town charm. If you enjoy outdoor recreation with a hankering for standing at the shore of a cool lake, with a fishing line in the water, this is the trip for you.

Routes & mileage: About 300 miles total, not including a side trip on the Rim Road. This loop tour begins in Payson, where you take State Route 87 north to Tonto Natural Bridge State Park, Pine, Strawberry, and Winslow. From Winslow, take Interstate 40 east to Holbrook. From there, U.S. Route 180 east leads you to the southern entrance of Petrified Forest National Park, which includes the Painted Desert. Return to Holbrook and take State Route 377 south to Heber, where you'll pick up State Route 260 west for the drive back to Payson.

Time to allow: Three days.

(LEFT) *A storm at sunset casts dramatic lighting on petrified logs and eroded clay formations at Blue Mesa in the Petrified Forest National Park.* JACK DYKINGA
(ABOVE, RIGHT) *Newspaper Rock bears a cluster of petroglyphs in the Petrified Forest National Park.* LARRY ULRICH
(RIGHT) *The Payson Rodeo, usually held around the Fourth of July, is one of the most famous, colorful, and oldest in the country.* PETER ENSENBERGER

Driving 10 miles north of Payson on State 87 brings you to Tonto Natural Bridge State Park. This mass of travertine straddling Pine Creek is believed to be the largest natural bridge in the world. It's 400 feet long, 183 feet high, and 150 feet wide. Visitors can enjoy the site from one of four overlooks, or by hiking into the canyon and looking back up.

The springs that deposited the limestone forming the bridge still flow from its peak onto moss-covered rocks below. These waterfalls are mesmerizing to watch, especially early in the morning. The park is often empty then and the canyon silent, except for the chatter of birds and the music of the tumbling water.

In 1927, David Gowan Goodfellow built a guest ranch on the site, attracting such notables as Teddy Roosevelt. The three-story lodge, now the park office, had 10 bedrooms, six with adjoining porches, and an observation deck converted from a sewing room. The deck offers a nice view of Pine Creek Canyon, a beautifully-manicured public picnic area adjacent to the lodge, and one of the original cabins Goodfellow rented to guests. In the 1930s, they went for the regal sum of 50 cents a night.

Drivers should know that the three-mile paved road leading from the highway to the park requires caution in wet or freezing weather. The entrance road snakes around tight turns and is steep (a 14 percent grade). In Goodfellow's day, the grade was 32 percent, and the road

(ABOVE AND LEFT) *Wildflowers grace the way to Tonto Natural Bridge, and moss-covered rocks adorn Pine Creek Falls. Both sites are in Tonto Natural Bridge State Park.* BOTH BY JERRY SIEVE
(OPPOSITE PAGE, TOP) *Members of the Strawberry community built this log schoolhouse in one day in 1885. Since being restored, it serves as a museum.*
(OPPOSITE, BOTTOM) *From the edge of the Mogollon Rim, the Tonto National Forest stretches for miles and miles.*
BOTH BY BOB & SUZANNE CLEMENZ

was not paved. He had departing guests drive their vehicles out in reverse, a gear with more power than forward gears. And in those days, fuel was fed to the engine through the front of the car by gravity. A vehicle going forward with, say, a quarter tank, would lose the flow of gas because it would slosh to the back of the tank, interrupting the gravity flow.

Pushing north on State 87, travelers soon begin climbing the Mogollon Rim, a term every Arizonan knows and every traveler should know. It's a giant, forested ledge that angles across the state for nearly 300 miles, forming the dividing line between the deserts and the high country. Mogollon (some people pronounce it Mow-ghee-YAWN; others say Muggy-OWN) means "obstruction" in Spanish, which it certainly was to early explorers trying to make their way north over rough and roadless terrain. Visitors might also hear it called the Tonto Rim. That's what Grey called it, figuring that was easier to remember — and to pronounce.

The highway takes you smack onto the Rim. Straddling the highway are Pine (elevation 5,400 feet) and Strawberry (elevation 6,800 feet), mountain hamlets that still retain their old-fashioned charm. Alongside the highway in Pine, a former chapel now houses one segment of the Pine Museum, which focuses on the pioneer era.

Don't pass through Strawberry without stopping at the Strawberry Lodge for a slice of homemade apple or buttermilk pie or having a look at the oldest standing schoolhouse in Arizona. Community residents threw together the log building in a single day in 1885. It closed 22 years later, due to a lack of students, and was roofless when it was saved from demolition in 1967. Located on Fossil Creek Road, Strawberry Schoolhouse now houses a second segment of the Pine Museum and you can picnic on the grounds.

Caution: Locals warn that it's dangerous to drive more than 30 mph at night on State 87, unless you want to risk getting cozy with an elk. In the forests north of Payson, their numbers have increased so dramatically that it's become almost common for speeding travelers to run into them on the curving, two-lane road. Elk have spindly legs, so the car flips them up and back through the windshield.

But in daytime, the highway is safe and fun. The 71-mile drive from Strawberry to Winslow starts out in the thick of the pines and rises over the Rim to the sage and shrub of the Colorado Plateau.

For a good but lengthy side trip, with some spectacular views, try the Rim Road. It is accessible 10 miles north of Strawberry, but that puts you on a rough section of road. Instead, continue on State 87 to the Coconino National Forest's Blue Ridge Ranger Station, 30 miles north of Strawberry. Just past the station, turn right onto Forest Service Road 95. It intersects the Rim Road (FR 300) in 19 miles. From there, continue on the better portion of the Rim Road another 33.5 miles and you emerge on State 260 about 17 miles east of Payson.

What sights does the Rim Road offer? No one could give a better description than Zane Grey. Consider this passage from *Under the Tonto Rim*:

"She gazed down on an endless green slope of massed treetops, across a rolling basin black with forest, to a colossal wall of red rock, level and black-fringed on top, but wildly broken along its face into gigantic cliffs, escarpments, points and ledges, far as the eye could see to east or west."

In Winslow, don't miss La Posada, one of America's great railroad hotels. The 68,000-square-foot mission-style building (larger than the Hearst Castle) opened in 1930 amid 16 acres of beautifully-tended gardens and groves of trees.

Over the years it hosted such notables as Harry Truman, Jimmy Stewart, Gary Cooper, Howard Hughes, and John Wayne, who was a regular during his film-making ventures into Monument Valley with director John Ford. "The Duke" would fly up to the Monument Valley in the morning, fly back when the work was done, then take over the hotel's Bull Ring Bar for the night. La Posada closed as a hotel in 1959, but reopened in 1998 after undergoing an extensive renovation.

Winslow has a rich aviation past, too. The local airport was designed by Charles Lindbergh, and Amelia Earhart once blacked out the town when her rear wheels caught on power lines during a takeoff from Lindbergh's airport. For more colorful stories of Winslow's past, including Route 66, frontier trading posts, and cowboys and Indians, visit the Old Trails Museum and its director, Janice Griffith, the unofficial keeper of legends.

Holbrook is 33 miles east of Winslow on I-40. If your visit is during the summer, enjoy the Indian dances on the plaza outside the Navajo County courthouse. While there, hop across the street to the Nakai Indian Center to watch an expert Native American silversmith at work, and for an after-dinner treat, try the fried ice cream at El Rancho Restaurant.

Holbrook is known as the hub city, a headquarters for day trips in the area. One of the most popular destinations, the Petrified Forest National Park, is only 19 miles out of town on U.S. 180. Start your tour of the Petrified Forest at the Rainbow Forest Museum, just past the southern

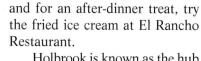

(LEFT) *Petrified logs in the Petrified Forest National Park seem to be resting on pedestals in the desert.* JACK DYKINGA
(ABOVE) *A motel on historic Route 66 at Holbrook features rooms shaped like tepees.* JAMES TALLON
(RIGHT) *Light filtered by clouds accentuates the colors soaked up in the flowing mounds of the Painted Desert.* GEORGE H.H. HUEY

entrance, and watch the short video explaining what the land was like some 220 million years ago, when it was a flood plain marked by streams, swamps, and 250-foot-tall trees. You'll also learn the process by which the wood turned to stone. The trees fell and were washed into swamps amid a packing of silt and clay that protected them from the decaying power of oxygen. Over millions of years, a mixture of volcanic ash and silica seeped into the wood, forming quartz crystals that slowly petrified the logs.

The drive through the park is 28 miles. Flanking the route are numerous vistas and hiking trails, including Crystal Forest, Agate Bridge, Blue Mesa, and the Tepees, a series of perfectly symmetrical cones that stand as testimony to nature's artistic power. Another site, Puerco Pueblo, occupied from A.D. 1250 to 1380, is an Indian ruin of some 100 rooms built around a large plaza. How interesting it is to stand amid this ancient development and have the deep silence broken by the howl of a Santa Fe

Railroad car shooting across the desert not a quarter mile behind you. The experience raises a question: What would the early residents of Puerco Pueblo have made of that?

Visitors to the Petrified Forest should be aware of the so-called curse that befalls those who illegally remove petrified wood from the park. Every year, park officials receive hundreds of letters and packages containing hunks of wood and heartfelt apologies from guilty souvenir hunters. These confessions include tales of disasters that have occurred since the theft, including deaths, headaches, hernias, wrenching guilt, and lousy luck in love.

A sample: "Take these miserable rocks and put them back . . . for they have caused pure havoc in my love life and Cheryl's, too. By the time these rocks reach you, things should be back to normal. If not, I give up. Signed — Dateless and Desperate."

At the north end of the park, near the junction with I-40, you'll find the Spanish-pueblo-style Painted Desert Inn,

(LEFT) Operations like the Brookbank Canyon Ranch west of Heber are scattered over the Mogollon Rim. JERRY JACKA

built in 1924. Today, it's a national landmark that serves as a museum, gift shop, and stopping point for travelers hoping to soak up the rich colors of the Painted Desert.

No excuse is acceptable for leaving the Painted Desert without first making your way from the inn to Kachina Point or to Chinde Point at sunset. Settle in on a picnic table and watch the stunning, Technicolor showcase of blues, grays, oranges, and lavenders that simply can't be found on any other landscape on earth.

From Holbrook, pick up State 377 south to Heber, a 41-mile drive on a two-lane road that makes you feel happily lonesome. In Heber, founded as a Mormon colony in 1876-77, you'll take State 266 for a drive through the Sitgreaves National Forest and some fine outdoor playgrounds, such as Christopher Creek, Kohl's Ranch, Forest Lakes, and Woods Canyon Lake.

The latter, a five-mile detour, includes the Woods Canyon Lake Store. This is a great spot for a picnic at the shore or to stock up on whatever supplies you might need for hiking, camping, hunting, or boating. Once back on State 260, the drive into Payson is pretty, especially on a fall morning, with yellow and red leaves dancing across the pavement and the shadows of the pines flickering over your windshield. 🔰

When You Go

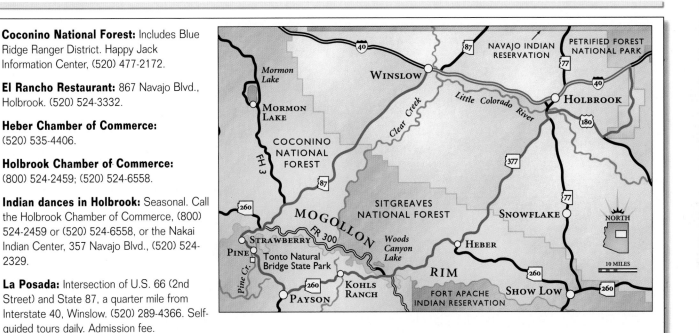

Coconino National Forest: Includes Blue Ridge Ranger District. Happy Jack Information Center, (520) 477-2172.

El Rancho Restaurant: 867 Navajo Blvd., Holbrook. (520) 524-3332.

Heber Chamber of Commerce: (520) 535-4406.

Holbrook Chamber of Commerce: (800) 524-2459; (520) 524-6558.

Indian dances in Holbrook: Seasonal. Call the Holbrook Chamber of Commerce, (800) 524-2459 or (520) 524-6558, or the Nakai Indian Center, 357 Navajo Blvd., (520) 524-2329.

La Posada: Intersection of U.S. 66 (2nd Street) and State 87, a quarter mile from Interstate 40, Winslow. (520) 289-4366. Self-guided tours daily. Admission fee.

Petrified Forest National Park: (520) 524-6228. Open 7:30 A.M. to 5 P.M. daily except Christmas and New Year's Day. Admission fee.

The Payson Candle Factory: 620 N. Beeline Highway, Payson. (520) 474-2152.

Pine/Strawberry Museum: (520) 476-3547. Open Monday through Saturday all year; closed Sunday, mid-October to mid-May. Call for hours and holiday closures.

Rim Country Regional Chamber of Commerce: Payson, (520) 474-4515 or (800) 672-9766. Pine-Strawberry, (520) 476-3547.

Sitgreaves National Forest: Black Mesa Ranger District, Overgaard. (520) 289-2471.

The Strawberry Lodge: (520) 476-3333. Open Monday through Thursday, 7 A.M. to 7 P.M.; Friday and Saturday, 7 A.M. to 8 P.M.

Strawberry Schoolhouse: (520) 476-3095. Open weekends, May through September. To arrange off-season group tours, call (520) 476-4791 or 476-3375.

Tonto Natural Bridge State Park: (520) 476-4202. Open 9 A.M. to 6 P.M., April through October; 9 A.M. to 5 P.M., November through March. Closed Christmas and whenever the entrance road is too icy. Admission fee. No pets. Free tours of the lodge on Saturday and Sunday, 11:30 A.M. and 2:30 P.M. (donations accepted).

Winslow Chamber of Commerce: (520) 289-2434.

Winslow's Old Trails Museum: 212 Kinsley Ave. (520) 289-5861. Tuesday to Saturday, 1 P.M. to 5 P.M. November through February, open Tuesday, Thursday, Friday, and Saturday, 1 P.M. to 5 P.M. Free.

Zane Grey Museum: 503 W. Main St., Payson. (520) 474-6243. Open 10 A.M. to 3 P.M. Monday through Saturday; Sunday 12 P.M. to 4 P.M. Admission fee.

A Lesson on Arizona's Diversity

DESERT TO MOUNTAINS TO MEADOWS

by Leo Banks

Beginning in the Gila County mining town of Globe, follow the combined U.S. Route 60/State Route 77 northeast through a sliver of the Tonto National Forest and into Apache country.

After 35 miles, the highway curls into a deep gorge known as the Salt River Canyon. At the right time of day, the play of the sun turns the rock walls red and purple, a sight made more dramatic as the surrounding ridge lines rise, the car radio fades, and you begin to feel as if you've dropped to the earth's bottom. In a way you have, so enjoy it. Stand at the bridge over the Salt River and listen to the rush of water tumbling over the rocks. The sound has a way of shoving life's burdens into the background.

For the adventurous, several outfitters offer one-day and multi-day rafting trips from this point down the Salt River during the spring runoff. For a listing of outfitters, check under the heading "river trips" in the US West Yellow Pages for Phoenix.

About 25 miles past the canyon, at Carrizo, U.S. 60/77 intersects with State Route 73, which loops eastward through the Fort Apache Indian Reservation, the home of the White Mountain Apache people. U.S. 60/70 continues its climb over the Mogollon Rim and into the White Mountains and the resort towns of Show Low, Pinetop, and Lakeside.

Those who thrill to the bugle call of Western history shouldn't miss Fort Apache Historic Park, located just off State Route 73. The fort, a key outpost in the Indian wars, was established in 1870 and operated until 1922. More than 20 buildings stand along Officer's Row, a tree-shrouded lane that once contained rows of huts and tents. The oldest standing structure is the recently refurbished cabin once occupied by General George Crook, commander of the Military Department of Arizona. The site also holds the Theodore Roosevelt School, which opened in 1923 with only Navajo students. Its central educational principal was to "take the Indian out of the Indian." Today it is a thriving boarding school for students of many tribes.

Another attraction is the new White Mountain Apache Cultural Center — known in Apache as *Nohwike' Bagowa*, "House of Our Footprints." It features a gift shop and museum exhibits explaining aspects of tribal culture. Just behind the center, walk the rocky trail that wends down the banks of the White River to a reconstructed Apache village. The hike requires about 10 minutes and takes you over a six-foot-wide footbridge, without side rails, that vibrates as you amble across.

Towns and sites: Globe, Salt River Canyon, White Mountains, Show Low, Fort Apache, Whiteriver, Hawley Lake, Sunrise Park Resort, Eagar, Springerville, Alpine, Hannagan Meadow, Clifton, Morenci, Safford, and San Carlos Indian Reservation.

Overview: This tour presents a picturesque primer on the state's astonishing variety of landscape and climate conditions, both of which can change from morning to afternoon with a few hours of driving. As you make your way from hilly desert to pure alpine meadows, and back to desert, ask yourself: Am I really in Arizona?

Routes & mileage: About 550 miles, including a trip to Show Low. Take the combined U.S. Route 60/State Route 77 from Globe through the Salt River Canyon; State Route 73 to Fort Apache, Whiteriver, and Hon Dah; State Route 260 west to Show Low and then back to Hon Dah and continue east to Eagar and Springerville; U.S. Route 191 south to Clifton and onto U.S. Route 70 to Safford and Globe.

Time to allow: Three days.

(OPPOSITE PAGE) *Framed by saguaro cactuses, the Salt River meanders lazily through the Salt River Canyon Wilderness in Central Arizona.* JACK DYKINGA
(ABOVE) *During the spring runoff, the Salt River becomes a white water playground for rafting.* JIM MARSHALL
(TOP) *Wild iris adorn a field at Hannagan Meadow, one of Arizona's premier mountain retreats.* EDWARD McCAIN

Standing amid the brush huts, with the wind whistling through the rocks of the bluff nearby, it's easy imagine that you're back in the days of Geronimo and General Crook.

The same is true at the old Fort Apache Cemetery, final resting place for many of the White Mountain Apache scouts whose service to Crook hastened the end of hostilities.

Their small, faded-white headstones bear no year of birth or death, no regiment, not even a complete name. A stone might say simply, "Bonita — Indian Scout." But we can assume that was enough for those who knew him.

The White Mountain Apache capital of Whiteriver is four miles beyond the fort on State 73. Visitors interested in experiencing Apache culture can attend the sunrise dances, generally held every weekend during the summer. The four-day, outdoor ceremonies mark a young woman's passage into adulthood. They include singing, dancing in full costume and paint, and feasting on traditional dishes, such as boiled hominy, acorn soup, and corn meal. The dances are open to the public. Be respectful. Don't take pictures without first checking with the medicine man directing the dance.

Those interested in exploring the reservation's backcountry should obtain permits at the tribe's outdoor recreation office, also in Whiteriver. Some 800 miles of streams and 26 lakes have earned this 1.7-million-acre preserve a reputation as a vacation paradise. If your dream getaway involves hauling native Apache trout from a pristine stream, or listening to the bugling of an elk while hiking through a forest shaded by autumn's orange, few spots are better. The tribe even offers groups the opportunity to rent a lake for a specific occasion. Many outdoor activities require an Apache tribal permit, not a state permit. Be sure to check before setting out.

Don't leave the reservation without stopping at Hon Dah Casino, 18 miles north of Whiteriver at the junction of state routes 73 and 260. Inside the casino, study the historic photos of Apache warriors and others lining the wall behind the cashier's window. Then lower your eyes just a few feet to the automatic coin-wrap machines shooting out rolls of quarters faster than you can blink. Now ask yourself: Which century am I in?

From Hon Dah, State Route 260 takes you off the reservation to Pinetop-Lakeside and Show Low, 16 miles to the west.

Show Low has an interesting story to tell. Back in the 1870s, pioneer-cattlemen Corydon E. Cooley and Marion Clark decided to end their partnership with a card game. "Show low and you win," said Clark. Cooley flipped a deuce, winning the ranch the two had started and giving a name to the quaint town that sprouted there.

Now, return via State 260 to Hon Dah and continue eastward for about 11 miles to State Route 473 and a short drive south to Hawley Lake, a reservoir built and operated by the Apaches. The lake offers fine fishing, rental cabins, camping, and, at 8,500 feet elevation, cool summer weather.

About nine miles past that turnoff, State Route 273 leads south to the White Mountain tribe's Sunrise Park Resort, a place where you can ski, fish, and enjoy fall colors.

With 65 runs on three mountains, Sunrise is one of the Southwest's finest skiing spots, featuring separate areas for snow-boarders, cross country trails, and a special ski-wee place for kids.

The 100-room Sunrise Hotel, located on the shore of

Sunrise Lake, makes this a prime spot for warm weather outings, too. The lake has a marina for boat rentals.

On special occasions during the summer, such as when the park hosts mountain bike races, and for viewing fall colors, the ski lifts open to the public. For $5, visitors can ride to the rustic lodge at the 11,000-foot peak of Apache Mountain for lunch in a breathtaking setting. Call ahead to learn exact dates and times.

Much of the White Mountains lies off the Apache reservation, and many who explore these portions use the twin towns of Eagar and Springerville as hubs. The first settlers called the region Valle Redondo, or Round Valley. One of the area's newest recreational possibilities is called Rails to Trails, a U.S. Forest Service project which transformed 20 miles of old railroad bed into a hiking and horseback riding course. Forest officials promise to double the trail's length in coming years.

The trail starts 18 miles west of Springerville on State 260, ranges past two lakes with boat rental facilities and general stores, and crosses a quaint 100-foot-long footbridge that one local jokes is only wide enough for a fat horse. The best of this trek is what you're likely to see on the way — deer, brown bear, soaring hawks.

A must-stop in downtown Eagar, population 4,000, is 4th Avenue's Vintage Hideaway, a combination breakfast and lunch spot, bakery, tea room, and upstairs gift shop. It's located in an elegant home built in 1932 by Hank and Bessie Brawley. But before they completed it, the Brawleys sold out to Geneva and Milford Wiltbank. Sale price: 15 cows and some lumber. If your visit is in the fall, you'll know the house by the grapevine that turns the entire north wall of the building red.

For those who like hunting for offbeat gifts, try the General Store Antique Mall on Main Street in

(LEFT) *Spectacular views dominate the runs at Sunrise Park Resort, owned and operated by the White Mountain Apache Tribe.* DON B. STEVENSON
(ABOVE) *The Black River near Alpine.* RICHARD MAACK

Springerville. Terry Tieman started the business after 25 years as a truck driver. He now has 13 antique dealers under one roof. "Most of our sellers grew up somewhere else, and they do their buying when they return home to visit," says Tieman. "So we have a variety of collectibles from all over."

The next leg of the tour runs south from Springerville to Clifton along U.S. 191, also known as the Coronado Trail. The road is named after Spanish explorer Francisco Vasquez de Coronado, who roamed this area more than 450 years ago in his futile search for the fabled Seven Cities of Cibola.

The road is a twisting, gasp-worthy, mostly guard-rail-free stretch of adventure that runs for 120 miles through the Apache National Forest. It takes three to four hours to drive — more in winter, assuming it's passable at all. At road level, elevation on this drive ranges from 9,100 to

3,000 feet as it passes through grassy meadows; forests of spruce, fir, and ponderosa pine; mountain lakes; and woodlands of piñon and juniper.

At its highest points, the trail curls through an area known as Arizona's Alps. This includes the town of Alpine, at the east end of the White Mountains and six miles from the New Mexico border, a place of rapid weather changes and incomparable beauty. Imagine a snow-packed hillside coming alive with white and yellow wildflowers as spring unfolds. Or spotting a black-eyed buck deer, steam shooting out his nostrils, staring at you through a stand of tall aspens in the dead of January.

Beyond Alpine is Hannagan Meadow, elevation 9,100 feet, named for a Nevada miner who ran a cattle ranch there in the 1870s. The lodge at the meadow was built in 1926 to accommodate travelers who needed a

(OPPOSITE PAGE, ABOVE) *Lodges cater year-round to White Mountain recreationists. Pictured is Greer Lodge, which features trout ponds on the property.* RICHARD MAACK
(OPPOSITE PAGE, BELOW) *Mount Baldy lies in the distance beyond Big Lake, a popular fishing water.* RANDY PRENTICE
(ABOVE) *New Mexican locust blooms amid aspen in the Blue Range Primitive Area.* JACK DYKINGA

break in what was then a two-day trek down to Clifton. The old building was renovated in 1996 and has dining facilities. Authentic log cabins, each with its own character and decor, are available for rent, as are skis, snowshoes, and snowmobiles. Ski instructors and guides are also on hand.

Drive seven miles beyond Hannagan Meadow to the

Blue Vista overlook. This spot looks out over the Blue Range Primitive Area, a little-known and still-wild parcel encompassing 187,000 acres. It's the last remaining primitive area in the national forest system, accessible only to the heartiest souls. For a kick, check out the arrow tree, less than a half mile past the overlook on the left. It's a snag pine (dead, branchless) into which local hunters every year shoot hundreds of arrows as target practice. It makes for a nice break in a drive that locals like to joke about. They say that when you're absolutely certain you've seen your last switchback, you're only halfway down the Coronado Trail.

The highway curls down into Morenci and the second largest open pit copper mine in America. Ore was discovered there in 1869, and in later decades the pit grew so big, it enveloped the entire town. A second Morenci sprang up, joining its sister community on the San Francisco River. Clifton is known for the territorial look of the buildings along its Chase Creek District, where outlaws once prowled the Old West saloons and made the nights exciting.

U.S. 191 joins U.S. 70 about 10 miles east of Safford for the tour's final leg back to Globe. Visitors can enjoy camping, picnicking, boating, fishing, and hot springs bathing at Roper Lake State Park, six miles outside town.

Another option is making your way to the 10,700-foot peak of the great green presence that hulks over the desert around Safford — Mount Graham. An 11-acre lake decorates the mountaintop, one of the highest spots in the state reachable by car.

The highway then rolls back into Apache land, past the settlements of Geronimo, Ft. Thomas, and Peridot, home of the new San Carlos Apache Cultural Center. It opened in September, 1995, and features a gift shop, exhibits, and promised for the future, shows by local artists. The last stop, 20 miles outside Globe, is the grand and glittering Apache Gold Casino. ◪

(ABOVE, LEFT AND RIGHT) *Clifton's Chase Creek District retains its territorial look.* RICHARD MAACK (LEFT) *Bonita Creek near Safford poses ideal conditions for viewing birds and wildlife.* DAVID H. SMITH (OPPOSITE PAGE) *Roper Lake State Park, which attracts campers, anglers, and picnickers, is nestled in a valley below Mount Graham near Safford.* TOM DANIELSEN

When You Go

Nohwike Bagowa/Apache Cultural Center and Museum: Fort Apache, (520) 338-4625. Open 8 A.M. to 5 P.M., Monday through Friday. Call for holiday hours and exhibit schedules. Admission fee.

Walking tours of Fort Apache: Contact Fort Apache Museum, (520) 338-1392, to make appointment. Admission fee.

Apache tribal information: For reservation permits, contact the tribe's Wildlife and Outdoor Recreation Division, Whiteriver, (520) 338-4385. For information on sunrise dances, contact the tribe's Office of Tourism, Fort Apache, (520) 338-1230.

Sunrise Park Resort: McNary. (800) 772-7669 or (520) 735-7600/7669. Web site: *www.sunriseskipark.com/*

Rails to Trails route: Contact the Springerville Ranger District, (520) 333-4372.

4th Avenue's Vintage Hideaway: 389 North Eagar St., Eagar. Open Monday to Thursday, 7 A.M. to 3 P.M.; Friday to Saturday, 7 A.M. to 8:30 P.M. (520) 333-4398.

The General Store Antique Mall: 173 West Main St., Springerville. 10 A.M. to 5 P.M., Monday to Saturday. (520) 333-5955.

Hannagan Meadow Lodge: Alpine. (520) 339-4370. Diners should make reservations.

Apache National Forest: Springerville, (520) 333-4372. Alpine Ranger District, (520) 339-4384.

Alpine Chamber of Commerce: (520) 339-4330.

Morenci mine tours: No charge; given by appointment on weekdays. (520) 865-1180 or (800) 882-1291.

Clifton and Morenci: Greenlee County Chamber of Commerce, Clifton. (520) 865-3313.

Roper Lake State Park: Four miles south of Safford off U.S. Route 191. Natural hot springs. Admission fee. (520) 428-6760.

To reach Mount Graham: Drive nine miles south of Safford on U.S. 191 and turn right onto State 366, called Swift Trail.

San Carlos Apache Cultural Center: Milepost 272, U.S. Route 70, in Peridot. Admission fee. For schedule, call (520) 475-2894.

Besh-Ba-Gowah Archaeological Park: Globe. Museum and Salado Indian ruins. Admission fee. (520) 425-0320.

A Trail Back Through Time

SEDONA, PRESCOTT, AND VERDE VALLEY   CENTRAL

by Leo Banks

The pleasant, uphill drive from Phoenix toward the Verde Valley on Interstate 17 passes a number of road signs — Black Canyon City, Horsethief Basin — that surely will inspire curiosity. Behind every one of them hangs a story. If time isn't a problem, and you're feeling adventuresome, travel the 26 miles of rough, curving, oh-my-gawd dirt road up the side of the Bradshaw Mountains to Bumble Bee and Crown King, population 65, and its famed old saloon.

The bar stood up its first shot glass about 1895 in the mining town of Oro Belle, eight miles away. Then it was pulled apart, board by board, and hauled on a wagon road to its present home and nailed back together. It has stayed put since 1916. If that story isn't worth a glass of beer, what is?

Back on I-17, the first eye-popping vista comes 90 miles north of Phoenix as you top the mountains and gaze over the grand, colorful, panoramic Verde Valley, home to Fort Verde State Historic Park, which preserves Camp Verde. The fort, completed in 1873, played a key role in winning the Apache wars.

Another well-preserved valley landmark, Montezuma Castle National Monument, is considered one of the Southwest's best Indian ruins. Ninety percent of the castle — actually, a series of rooms set in the cavelike recesses of a cliff — is original, which means you're seeing almost exactly what the Sinagua people built some 875 years ago. The site is so well preserved because the lip of the cliff extends 10 feet beyond the dwelling itself, preventing heavy monsoon rain from washing away the mortar or rotting roof timbers.

"People are amazed at how high it is, and they want to know why in the world did they built it so high," says Ranger Barbara Prewitt. "Because that's where the cave is. They wanted a roof over their head." Visitors view the castle from below — binoculars are helpful — but are not allowed inside. A full tour of the site takes only 20 minutes.

Towns & sites: Crown King (optional), Verde Valley, Fort Verde State Historic Park, Montezuma Castle and Tuzigoot national monuments, Sedona, Cottonwood, Clarkdale, Jerome, Prescott, Skull Valley, and Wickenburg.

Overview: If you want to slow down life's pace for a few days, head to Central Arizona valleys and mountains and a trip back through Arizona's pre-history and its Old West era, as well as a combination of the two found in places like Sedona. Keep your eyes open: On this tour you're likely to spot a cowboy, his boot resting on the back bumper of a pickup, talking on a cellular phone.

Routes & mileage: About 375 miles, including a side trip to Crown King. From Phoenix, take Interstate 17 north to Exit 248 and the side trip to Crown King. Back on I-17, continue north to Exit 287 for Camp Verde. Take Exit 289 and follow the signs to Montezuma Castle (follow the signs). Back on I-17, drive north to Exit 298 (State Route 179) and a 15-mile drive north to Sedona. From there, take State Route 89A south to Cottonwood, Clarkdale, and Jerome. Continue south on State 89A to 89 and south to Prescott. From Prescott, take Iron Springs Road to Skull Valley, Kirkland, and Kirkland Junction, where you intersect with State 89 and a 36-mile drive south to Wickenburg. From there, take U.S. 60 to State Route 74, east to Interstate 17, and south to Phoenix.

Time to allow: Two to three days.

(LEFT) *Sacred datura blooms at Montezuma Castle, a cliff dwelling built some 875 years ago by the Sinagua people.*
RICHARD MAACK
(ABOVE, RIGHT) *Cavalry re-enactments at Fort Verde State Historic Park tell the story of frontier days.*
(RIGHT) *Cottonwoods line the tranquil Verde River south of old Fort Verde near the supply trail built by General Crook during the Apache wars.* BOTH BY NICK BEREZENKO

Eleven miles away is Montezuma Well, a limestone sink-hole and spring. Ruins remain in the cliff along one side of the well. A trail leads alongside the well to its outlet, where the water goes under a mountain and into a creek on the other side. On most days, a storyteller roams the vicinity. Imagine yourself hearing the legend called Apache Tears while enjoying lunch under the cottonwoods.

Only a few miles separate aboriginal Arizona from the New Age and other attractions of Sedona.

If you've never seen Sedona before, the red rocks will force a double take from you. They're beyond beautiful and, in the thinking of some, powerful. Do they actually promote peace, harmony, and a high, healing energy? The notion that they do has spread around the world and made Sedona into a mecca for seekers of every stripe.

Expect to encounter ideas you've never run into before, such as aura photography and hands-on energy healing. You can also take a psychic bus tour. Wouldn't it be nice? If there were problems with your reservation, you would know in advance.

But Sedona has much more than good vibes. Topping the attractions list are outstanding art galleries, shopping, chi-chi resorts, tennis, golf, balloon rides, jeep and helicopter tours of the back country, and two state parks — Red Rock and Slide Rock. The latter, a natural water slide in Oak Creek, seven miles north of town on State 89A, is a good and safe place to let the kids work off energy.

(OPPOSITE PAGE, ABOVE) *Serenity dominates the West Fork of Oak Creek Canyon in the Red Rock-Secret Mountain Wilderness north of Sedona.* DAVID MUENCH
(BELOW) *The rugged splendor of red rock country unfolds from Schnebly Hill Road.* KERRICK JAMES
(RIGHT, ABOVE) *Gleeful shouts resonate from thrill seekers plunging down a natural water slide at Slide Rock State Park on Oak Creek.* JEFF KIDA
(RIGHT, BELOW) *Sinagua Plaza, in uptown Sedona along State 89A, harbors a more relaxed style of whiling away time, shopping, and visiting galleries.* TOM BEAN

Jeep excursions range from the simple to the strenuous. For example, Sedona Red Rock Jeep Tours offers one in which travelers, accompanied by a guide, canoe down the shallow rapids of the Verde River to a series of limestone caves once inhabited by the Sinaguans. Visitors come ashore and hike into the caves.

As for Sedona's shopping, the spectrum is wide. But expect the unusual. "People want to buy something more than a tomahawk and a T-shirt," says Kim Coffey, a clerk at Looking West, a clothing, jewelry, and gift shop on State 89A. "They want something they can't get in Michigan, like a traditional Navajo broomstick skirt or a tapestry vest in a Southwestern design."

Leaving Sedona, follow State 89A south for 19 miles to Cottonwood and its sister town of Clarkdale. Both are

booming with an influx of retirees drawn by the temperate climate and small-town charm.

The area boasts the Tuzigoot National Monument, a Sinaguan pueblo perched on a 120-foot ridge, and the popular Verde Canyon Railroad. Its open-air, gondola-style cars make it a great way to see what's out there, whether it's bald eagles, buzzards, or a deer bounding through the brush. The train boards in Clarkdale and traverses 40 miles of Arizona outback, including the Sycamore Wilderness, over the four-hour journey.

To keep the fun going into the night, try the Blazin' M Ranch for a chuckwagon supper and stage show consisting of western singing, music, and comedy. The ranch is a collection of Old West buildings next to Dead Horse Ranch State Park. The quaint setting houses several specialty shops, a sarsaparilla bar, petting farm, horseshoe pits, and shooting gallery.

From Clarkdale, drive four miles into the mountains to Jerome, a favorite of those who believe in the impossible. The little town clings to the steep slopes of Cleopatra Hill in a way that seems to defy gravity. It was founded as a mining camp in 1876, and in the almost 125 years since, it has survived devastating fires, depressions in the copper market, and in the early 1950s, when the mines closed for good, abandonment.

(LEFT) *Nostalgia and terrific scenery await those who take the Verde Canyon Railroad four-hour, 40-mile excursion.* (BELOW) *The pueblo ruins at Tuzigoot National Monument crown a 120-foot ridge alongside the Verde River where Sinagua people lived.* BOTH BY BOB & SUZANNE CLEMENZ (OPPOSITE PAGE, LEFT) *The Verde River forms the centerpiece for Dead Horse Ranch State Park near Cottonwood with the Black Hills as a backdrop.* JERRY JACKA (OPPOSITE PAGE, RIGHT) *Now an artists community, Jerome still offers glimpses of its historic past.* JAMES TALLON (OPPOSITE PAGE, BOTTOM) *Houses perch precariously on pads dug into Jerome's Cleopatra Hill.* GEORGE H.H. HUEY

shops, restaurants, and some first-class bed-and-breakfast inns.

Don't miss the Douglas mansion, better known as the Jerome State Historic Park. It was built by James S. Douglas, made wealthy by the tons of copper pulled from the mountainside. The mansion contains exhibits explaining the mining life and rooms displaying period furniture and decoration.

The Jerome Grand Hotel is a story in itself. The building was built as a hospital in 1926 by United Verde Copper Co. The hospital shut down in 1950, and for the next 34 years, the building sat unused, collecting dust and spirits.

But beginning in the 1960s, it was reclaimed by poets, artists, and other dreamers who believed they could remake what had been a to-hell-with-tomorrow boomtown. They've succeeded. Today, the corkscrew streets of old Jerome, population 470, are lined with antique and gift

To former Phoenix entrepreneur Larry Altherr, and his brother and sister-in-law, Bob and Deb Altherr, it was a hotel waiting to happen. "The way the building was laid out, making it into a hotel was not that hard," Larry says. "Besides, if you want to move to a place like Jerome, you have to invent your own job."

Their "invention," unlikely as it seems, is a beauty, with its 1950s-style telephone switchboard, graceful copper fixtures, and from its restaurant, a truly breathtaking view of the Verde Valley, including the San Francisco Peaks and the red rocks.

But for Altherr, one of the best parts of running the Grand View is hearing the stories told by Jerome old-timers who return to say hello. One lady, after checking in, came down to the front desk with an astonished look. She told the clerk that she gave birth to her daughter in that very same room, some 50 years before.

From the Grand Hotel, continue up the hill on State 89A. Be prepared to negotiate some devilish switchbacks as you climb Mingus Mountain, topping out at more than 7,700 feet. After 25 miles, the road joins State 89 for the short drive into Prescott.

Fifty years ago, this former territorial capital was, in the words of one long-time Prescott resident, "as good a cowboy town as you'd ever find." The cowboys are still evident, but these days their boots are shiny, their Stetsons don't have sweat rings, and they're dining on salmon and salads at the Palace Saloon along legendary Whiskey Row.

Any visit to Prescott should start at the downtown square, anchored by the Yavapai County Courthouse, a great and grand building surrounded by grass, sculptures, trees, and a good bit of Arizona history.

Dentist-turned-gambler Doc Holliday had a run of

extraordinary luck at the gaming tables of Whiskey Row, just west of the courthouse, before heading to Tombstone to play his role in the O.K. Corral shoot-out. Virgil Earp, Wyatt's older brother, lived in Prescott before and after the 1881 gunfight, mining and running a sawmill. More recently, Barry Goldwater announced his successful candidacy for the Republican Party's 1964 presidential nomination on the courthouse square.

Prescott's story is best told at two of its museums.

The Sharlot Hall Museum, named for one of Arizona's earliest and most distinguished writers and historians, is on Gurley Street three blocks west of the square. Its immaculately tended grounds include the refurbished home of the territory's first governor, a gift shop, museum, and first-class research library.

The Smoki Museum (pronounced smoke-eye) is another frequently overlooked treasure. The unique stone and wood structure, built by federal Work Projects Administration workers and opened in 1935, contains a

wealth of artifacts collected from Indian archaeological sites in northern Arizona. The museum's founder, famed archaeologist Byron Cummings, believed that articles belonging to the ancients of Arizona should stay in Arizona. Smoki's collection includes baskets, pottery, beadwork, jewelry, stone effigies, and kachina dolls.

For a gander at Prescott's living past that doesn't require leaving the car, drive down Mount Vernon or Union street and see all the elegant Victorian homes that have been refurbished to their early splendor.

Most travelers stay on State 89 when leaving Prescott. But for a scenic side trip that adds only a few miles, take Iron Springs Road (Yavapai County Road 10) through Skull Valley. The town is a picturesque treat with six buildings, including a cafe and old-style general store.

Yavapai 10 continues past Kirkland and onto State 89. The highway rolls through the lush grasslands of the Peeples Valley and past a thoroughbred horse farm that looks like something out of the old TV show *Dallas*. Look out for Yarnell Hill, which makes a doozy of a drop as it

(OPPOSITE PAGE, TOP) *Once lined with saloons, Prescott's Whiskey Row offers a variety of shops and restaurants.* (OPPOSITE PAGE, BOTTOM) *Prescott's history and culture center on the Yavapai County Courthouse Square.* (ABOVE) *Despite Prescott's frontier heritage, Victorian-style houses form a district near downtown. Some have been made into bed-and-breakfast inns.* ALL BY RICHARD MAACK (RIGHT) *A family enjoys a hike in the Granite Mountain Wilderness near Prescott.* EDWARD McCAIN

snakes its way down the mountains to the desert floor. In Yarnell, take a few minutes for a drive one-half mile west of State 89 to visit the Shrine of St. Joseph of the Mountains. The shrine contains a trail leading to each of the 14 Stations of the Cross with life-size statuary set into a hillside.

Next stop: Wickenburg. For decades now, the town has been known as the dude ranch capital of Arizona. On the way into town on State 89, you'll see a sign for Griff's Wickenburg Inn. The Griff in question is Merv Griffin, creator of the *Jeopardy* and *Wheel of Fortune* TV shows.

Wickenburg also offers a historic walking tour of downtown and a number of quality galleries and shops. If your visit is in springtime, drive out to the Joshua tree forest 30 miles northwest of town. The beauty of the trees in bloom is overwhelming.

A word you'll see often in Wickenburg is Hassayampa. Amaze your friends by explaining to them its meaning in Apache. In rough translation, it's "river which runs upside

(ABOVE) *Skull Valley offers pastoral scenes on the outskirts of an old-style village and general store.* MICHAEL COLLIER
(LEFT) *Hiking is easy and pleasant in the Hassayampa River Preserve on the southern edge of Wickenburg.*
(OPPOSITE PAGE) *Wickenburg's Gold Rush Days features a parade and other festivities.* BOTH BY EDWARD McCAIN

down," for those portions of the Hassayampa River — actually most it — that flow underground.

On the way out of town on U.S. 60, you pass the Hassayampa River Preserve. In this lush hideaway, the river is above ground, flowing clear and beautiful through the desert. The Nature Conservancy manages the preserve and offers free, guided walks.

For the tour's last leg, Wickenburg to Phoenix, take U.S. 60 to State 74 for a drive past an excellent stand of saguaro cactus and Lake Pleasant. The lake complex includes a county park with camping, picnicking, and boat launching facilities, and spots from which to shore fish.

When You Go

Blazin' M Ranch: (520) 634-0334 or (800) WEST643. Cottonwood, past entrance to Dead Horse Ranch State Park.

Bumble Bee and Crown King: Follow the road from I-17 all the way up. The road might not be drivable in wet weather. For road conditions, call the Prescott National Forest work center at Crown King, (520) 632-7740, or Yavapai County Road Department, (520) 771-3177. The saloon's phone number is (520) 632-7053.

Coconino National Forest: Sedona Ranger Station, (520) 282-4119.

Cottonwood-Verde Valley Chamber of Commerce: (520) 634-7593.

Dead Horse Ranch State Park: (520) 634-5283. From Clarkdale, take Tuzigoot Road to 5th Street and turn south. From Cottonwood, take State 89A (Cottonwood Street) to Main Street, which bears left 90 degrees after it crosses Mingus Avenue. Turn right onto 10th Street, cross the Verde River, and go about a mile to the park. Open for day use 8 A.M. to 8 P.M. Admission fee. Camping facilities include hookups. The park offers hiking, bird watching, picnicking, and fishing.

Fort Verde State Historic Park: (520) 567-3275. Open daily 8 A.M. to 4:30 P.M. Admission fee.

Hassayampa River Preserve: For guided walks, seasonal hours of operation, etc., (520) 684-2772. Donations requested.

Jerome Grand Hotel: 200 Hill St., Jerome. (520) 634-8200.

Jerome State Historic Park: (520) 634-5381. Open 8 A.M. to 5 P.M. daily, except Christmas. Admission fee.

Montezuma Castle National Monument: (520) 567-3322. Open daily 8 A.M. to 5 P.M. Admission fee. Take Exit 289 off the I-17 or, from Camp Verde, take Montezuma Castle Highway. Staff can direct you to Montezuma Well (no admission fee).

Red Rock State Park: (520) 282-6907.

Sedona Chamber of Commerce: (800) 288-7336.

Sedona Red Rock Jeep Tours: (800) 848-7728.

Sharlot Hall Museum: 415 W. Gurley St., Prescott. (520) 445-3122. No admission fee, but donation requested.

Slide Rock State Park: (520) 282-3034. Admission fee. Water quality hot line, (602) 542-0202 (check ahead for closures).

Smoki Museum: 147 N. Arizona St., Prescott. (520) 445-1230. Admission fee. Open weekdays April through October and weekends all year.

Tuzigoot National Monument: (520) 634-5564. 8 A.M. to 5 P.M. daily. Admission fee. From Clarkdale, go east on Broadway to Tuzigoot Road and drive 1.5 miles to the site.

Verde Canyon Railroad: (800) 293-7245. Boarding is at 300 N. Broadway, Clarkdale.

Wickenburg Chamber of Commerce: (800) 942-5242.

A Short Trip Through the Centuries

HISTORICAL SITES AND ANCIENT RUINS

by Leo Banks

Towns & sites: Mormon Church's Arizona Temple in Mesa, Superstition Mountains and Lost Dutchman State Park, Boyce Thompson Arboretum State Park, Globe-Miami, Tonto National Monument, Roosevelt Dam and Lake, Tonto National Forest, Punkin Center, and Jakes Corner.

Overview: This tour doesn't venture far from Phoenix, at least in terms of distance. But it offers a variety of natural and man-made attractions, along with a strong dose of history and Indian ruins. A part of the trip takes you over the Gila-Pinal Scenic Road.

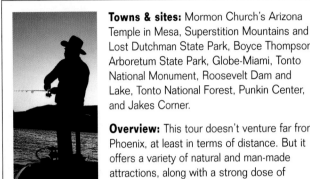

Routes & mileage: About 250 miles. From Interstate 10 in Phoenix, take U.S. Route 60 east to Globe. Then take State Route 88 to State 188 to State 87 and you're back in the Phoenix area.

Time to allow: One day.

Begin at U.S. 60, also known as the Superstition Freeway, and head east from Interstate 10. A good first stop, just a few miles out, is the Arizona Temple, spiritual home to members of the Church of Jesus Christ of Latter-day Saints. This majestic building, located in Mesa, is worth visiting year round, but especially during the Christmas season. From the day after Thanksgiving through December 31, the beautifully tended grounds glow with approximately 600,000 lights. They hang from the trees and shrubs, around the mirror pools and gardens, even from the 51 replicas of animals that decorate the property.

Every night during this stunning Festival of Lights, the temple hosts a show featuring Christmas music performed by junior high, high school, and college singers. It takes place outside under a canopy, and seating is almost always at capacity. The temple also hosts a massive Easter Pageant with some 400 actors in costume. It's held the week before Easter and draws 125,000 people in six days.

Back on U.S. 60, the highway rolls east past Mesa's and Gilbert's housing developments and golf courses until the Superstition Mountains appear on the eastern horizon over the retirement haven of Apache Junction. Pima Indians called them the "crooked top mountains" and told of the evil spirits that lived there. Any man who dared to venture into them was sure to disappear. The warning didn't deter a German immigrant named Jacob Waltz, nicknamed "the Dutchman." He'd disappear into the Superstitions and return with gold. Unfortunately, Waltz died before revealing the location of his find, which has set in motion a century of speculation, searching, and a few murder mysteries. It also created one of the West's great legends.

Travelers can follow in Waltz's footsteps at Lost Dutchman State Park. The site offers overnight camping, picnic areas, guided moonlight hikes, and campfire programs in which a volunteer shows a film, then takes guests outside to roast marshmallows and work a few theories about the whereabouts of Waltz's hidden bonanza. Day-use hiking is popular, too. If you're in good shape, try Siphon Draw Trail. It twists through a rocky outcropping, rising 2,000 feet to the pinnacle of a formation called the Flatiron. The round trip is 4.8 miles and in places the trail is hand-over-foot steep.

Continuing on the tour, 51 miles east of Phoenix is the Boyce Thompson Arboretum State Park. Plants from all over the world are exhibited in a 725-acre garden founded by William Boyce Thompson, who made his fortune mining

(OPPOSITE PAGE) *Lost Dutchman State Park affords an excellent view of the western end of the Superstition Mountains.* GEORGE STOCKING
(TOP) *A fisherman savors the moment on Apache Lake, along the Apache Trail in the Superstitions.* JAMES TALLON
(ABOVE) *A guide tells visitors about desert plants at the Boyce Thompson Arboretum State Park near Superior.* BOB & SUZANNE CLEMENZ

A Short Trip Through the Centuries 67

around Superior. He helped lead a Red Cross mercy mission to Russia after the revolution in 1917. What he saw convinced him that man and plants need one another for survival. Upon his return, he endowed the Boyce Thompson Institute for Plant Research at Cornell and the arboretum, dedicated in 1929.

Something is always in bloom there, no matter the season. Spring wildflowers grow everywhere on the grounds and are particularly popular. Numerous trails snake off from the visitors center, each providing a different experience. Walk the eucalyptus trail and stand in the shadows of these towering giants. It's a bit humbling to gaze to the top of a 160-foot-tall red gum eucalyptus, with a trunk measuring eight feet in diameter. The trail along Queen Creek is gorgeous and cool beneath the cottonwood, Arizona ash, and pecan trees.

One of the arboretum's attractions is the Curandero Trail. *Curandero* refers to traditional Mexican healers whose use of desert plants for curing illness goes back centuries. This hilly desert trail features 25 different plant species used by curanderos, with interpretive signs in English and Spanish.

Suffering from fever? Try tea made from the flowers of the Mexican elderberry. The juice of the prickly pear cactus is believed to be an effective treatment for adult-onset (insulin-resistant) diabetes. And snakeweed flowers, or the plant's leafy stems, diminish arthritis pain when added to a hot bath.

The trail offers a bit of a history lesson, too. Want to know how early settlers got along without a morning cup of Starbucks coffee? They plucked and dried the stems of a thin, green plant called Mormon tea and brewed them up. The result was a pleasant-tasting, mildly stimulating drink used as a coffee substitute.

The arboretum today is a serene place, guarded to the south by the imposing, saguaro-studded slope of Picket Post Mountain. But it wasn't always so peaceful. During the Indian wars, the mountain was the site of a military outpost and a lookout for soldiers charged with protecting early miners against Apache raids.

From saguaros to smokestacks, U.S. 60 continues east through the mining towns of Superior, Miami, and Globe. The latter has produced hundreds of millions of dollars worth of silver and copper since its founding in 1876. Legend has it that the town, originally Globe City, was named after the discovery of a 50-pound, globe-shaped silver nugget showing the outlines of the continents. As good as that tale is, it's probably false. Most believe the name derives from the first mining claim filed there, on September 19, 1873, called the Globe Ledge.

The modern town, population 7,000, still relies on mining for its economic base. But tourism is growing, too. The old county jail and sheriff's office have been refurbished and are open to visitors. They're downtown, right behind the old Gila County courthouse, which was completed in 1907 and remained in use until 1976. After eight years of inactivity and decay, the building was refurbished and now houses the Cobre Valley Center for the Arts.

Local painters display their work in the first-floor gallery, and in the basement, weavers sit at looms crafting colorful creations. Walk the grand staircase with its copper banisters to the second floor, where a theater group occupies what was once the courtroom. Across the hall is the office of the clerk of the Superior Court. At least that's what it says on the glass door. It's a little eerie to glance inside the virtually empty room these days and see the big black safe still in the wall behind a barefoot, leotard-clad woman practicing tai chi as mystical music plays on a tape deck. Times change, but not at the Gila County Historical Museum, housed in what was once the Globe-Miami Mine Rescue Station. Many are intrigued by the period look of the building's interior, built from 1919-1920, and the displays on the Indians, ranchers, and miners who inhabited the area.

The Besh-Ba-Gowah Archaeological Park, probably

(LEFT) *Besh-Ba-Gowah ruins in Globe: Ancient dwellers entered rooms by way of a ladder.* JERRY SIEVE
(OPPOSITE PAGE, TOP) *Salado people lived in this dwelling at Tonto National Monument.* ROBERT G. McDONALD
(OPPOSITE PAGE, BOTTOM) *The Salado also occupied this site, called the lower ruin at Tonto National Monument. An easily walked trail leads to the site.* GEORGE H.H. HUEY

dwellings at Tonto National Monument, located on the west side of the highway. The dwellings sit on a bluff 500 to 600 feet above the lake. From the parking area and visitors center, you'll hike a steep, winding paved trail to reach the ruins. The view from the two-story, 19-room pueblo is terrific. The cliffs hold another dwelling, with 40 rooms and three levels, accessible only by guided tour.

This hidden jewel of the Tonto Basin attracts a modest 72,000 visitors a year, many of whom want to know why the Salado didn't also build on the flatlands below the cliffs. Consider that question as you stand on the high bluff and gaze down across the purple desert to the water's edge. The answer is that they did. But those dwellings were consumed when the dam went in and are now under water.

"There was no protection for sites like this in those days," Monument Superintendent Lee Baiza says. "I guess we had different priorities then. Maybe 50 years from now someone will second guess what we're doing."

Many first-time Arizona travelers are amazed to see the perfect blue of the water sitting in a desert basin. The surprise grows at the sight of boats stacked up at the lakeshore marina. How the lake got there is a story of human bravery and engineering genius that bears retelling.

This 23-mile-long reservoir, originally called Tonto Lake, was formed with the construction of Roosevelt Dam between 1905 and 1911 to provide water storage and flood protection for the Salt River

Globe's best known attraction, has a period look, too, but of a thoroughly different variety. This ancient Salado Indian ruin, built between 600 and 700 years ago, took 225 years to build and once contained more than 200 rooms. Portions of the site have been reconstructed and some rooms are equipped with items the inhabitants used in everyday life. Visitors can prowl the rooms, climb ladders, and duck into the doorways. A small museum, housed in a former school building, and an educational video answer many questions about the Salado. But what happened to them remains a mystery.

"Nobody knows exactly why they left or where they went," says Park Manager Lynnette Brandon. "One theory is they had to move because of droughts throughout the Southwest about 1400 A.D." For a hundred years after its abandonment, the two-story pueblo was a ghost city, until the Apaches arrived. Besh-Ba-Gowah, in the Apache tongue, means "place of metal."

The tour moves northwest from Globe on State 88 to Tonto National Monument and Roosevelt Dam and Lake.

Before you come to the dam, visit the Salado cliff

Valley, which runs through Phoenix. In those days, the Tonto Basin was wild country. In order to get supplies and equipment to the site from Mesa, work crews had to forge a 60-mile road. It was completed in 1904, and within a year, 1.5 million pounds of freight were reaching Roosevelt every month by mule train.

Constructing the dam required more than 4,000 laborers, including Mexicans, Chinese, Apaches, and Italian stonemasons. They were paid $2 a day and lived in tents with cement floors, a stove, and a spring bed. More than 30 died during eight years of dangerous work, including the construction of the supply road. Among them was Al Sieber, who had become a legend in his years as chief of scouts during the Apache Wars. He survived many harrowing battles, but died at Roosevelt in 1907 when a boulder fell on him.

Today, Roosevelt Dam is 376 feet high and 184 feet thick at its base. The lake behind it is a summertime playground for heat-weary Phoenicians interested in boating, fishing, camping, hiking, piloting all-terrain vehicles, horseback riding, rock hounding, and hunting for gold.

"We've got quite a few prospectors out here," says Art Keeter, a ranger at the Forest Service visitors center at Roosevelt Lake. "One fellow has been here 40 years, making his bills every year just from the gold and gypsum he finds in the flatlands. He doesn't even go up in the mountains."

To understand how remote this area still is, Keeter recommends stopping at the gas station, 16 miles north of the lake at Butcher's Hook, and experiencing the portable potties out back. "That's how countrified we are," he says, smiling. "We have a Union 76 station with outhouses, one for men and one for women."

After inspecting the massive dam, pick up State 188 and head north past Punkin Center and the tiny crossroads settlement of Jakes Corner. Old West fans will surely spot the hitching posts in front of the wood frame buildings on the west side of the highway, just short of the intersection with State 87. That's the Jakes Corner Bar, a pretty good replica of a frontier saloon, and one of the last still operating in Arizona. The inside is stuffed with antiques, from a Montana mule harness to

(LEFT) *A lush hillside of saguaros, teddy bear cholla, and brittlebush slopes down to Roosevelt Lake at Tonto National Monument.* LARRY ULRICH (RIGHT) *Campers at Windy Hill Campground on Roosevelt Lake begin the day with a view of Four Peaks in the Mazatzal Mountains, a part of the Tonto National Forest.* RANDY PRENTICE

old guns, period photographs, and a classic wood stove.

The tour's final stretch follows State 87 south into Phoenix. This road curls like a family of rattlesnakes as it descends the Mazatzal Mountains and requires concentration to drive it. It eventually intersects with the turnoff to Saguaro Lake and the Salt River Recreation Area, popular fishing and boating spots, and it passes through a portion of the Fort McDowell Indian Reservation. ⊠

When You Go

Besh-Ba-Gowah Archaeological Park: (520) 425-0320. Globe. Located on Jess Hayes Road in the Globe Community Center complex, a mile and a quarter from downtown. Open 9 A.M. to 5 P.M. seven days a week, except Thanksgiving, Christmas, and New Year's days. Admission fee.

Boyce Thompson Arboretum State Park: (520) 689-2723; recording, (520) 689-2811. Three miles west of Superior on U.S. 60. Open seven days a week, except Christmas, 8 A.M. to 5 P.M. Admission fee.

Cobre Valley Center for the Arts: 101 N. Broad St., Globe. (520) 425-0884. Call for times that the Hand Weaving Studio is open.

Globe-Miami Chamber of Commerce: 1360 N. Broad St., Globe. (800) 804-5623 or (520) 425-4495. The Gila County Historical Museum, open Monday through Friday, 10 A.M. to 4 P.M., is at the same address. (520) 425-7385.

Lost Dutchman State Park: (480) 982-4485. Exit U.S. 60 at Idaho Road. Travel north to State 88 in Apache Junction, turn right, and drive five miles. Popular with RV campers, the park has no hookups, but does have shower buildings with hot water and accessible bathrooms. Admission fee.

Mormon Church's Arizona Temple: 525 E. Main St., Mesa. (480) 964-7164. Exit U.S. 60 at Mesa Drive. Go north (left) to Main Street, then east (right) to the visitors center. The visitors center is open seven days a week all year, but hours vary seasonally. Call for holiday event schedule.

Tonto National Forest: Supervisor's Office, Phoenix, (602) 225-5200; for information about Saguaro and Canyon lakes, call the

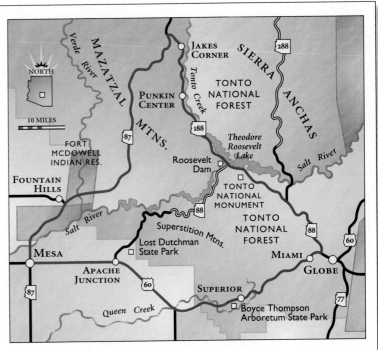

Mesa Ranger District, (480) 610-3300; Globe Ranger District, (520) 402-6200; Tonto Basin Ranger District, (520) 467-3200. Roosevelt Lake Visitors Center, Tonto Basin, (520) 467-2236, is open 7:45 A.M. to 4:30 P.M. seven days a week. Closed Thanksgiving, Christmas, and New Year's days.

Tonto National Monument: (520) 467-2241. Open from 8 A.M. to 5 P.M. seven days a week, except Christmas. The lower cliff dwelling is open to the public from 8 A.M. to 4 P.M.

Along the Lower Colorado River

YUMA AND WILDLIFE REFUGES

by Tom Dollar

I begin this trip where a lot of American Southwest history begins — the Yuma Crossing near the point at which the Colorado and Gila rivers once merged, before modern diversion dams altered their courses.

When Spanish explorers entered the region in 1540, they found Quechan Indian villages along these wide, untamed rivers. The Quechans grew melons, beans, corn, and pumpkins on the fertile floodplain. Missionaries followed on the heels of the Spanish soldiers. One of them, Father Eusebio Francisco Kino, mapped the confluence region and, with the help of Quechan guides, discovered an overland passage to the Pacific Ocean, thus proving that California was not an island.

Seventy-five years later, Captain Juan Bautista de Anza retraced Kino's route to the crossing, then proceeded into California and explored the San Francisco Bay area in 1776, the same year the United States of America was born. A missionary traveling with Anza, Father Francisco Garcés, crossed the Colorado and founded Mission La Purísima Concepcíon on a granite bluff that later became the site of Fort Yuma.

The historic saga continues. In the 1800s, mountain men passed through in their quest for beaver furs; the Mormon Battalion crossed at Yuma in 1847 during the Mexican War; and in the 1850s, thousands of gold rushers flooded to Yuma Crossing. To prevent ongoing hostilities between travelers and Indians, the U.S. Army established Fort Yuma in 1850 and set up the Yuma quartermaster depot on the opposite bank. Steamboats delivered supplies upriver from the Gulf of California to the depot at Yuma Crossing, and from there, goods were distributed to U.S. military installations throughout the Southwest, including Nevada, Utah, New Mexico, and Texas.

Military presence at the crossing brought the stability necessary for a townsite to grow and flourish. In 1854, the year Arizona became a territorial possession of the United States, the town of Colorado City was mapped across the river from Fort Yuma. Its name was changed in 1858 to Arizona City and finally to Yuma in 1873 (a different Colorado City still exists in northern Arizona). The town's first big building project was the Yuma Territorial Prison, a federal prison intended to serve the entire Southwest.

Today, stepping back in time at the Yuma Crossing State Historic Park, I wander through buildings and exhibits preserved on the grounds. The transportation storehouse features, among other things, a wonderfully preserved Butterfield mail coach, grain wagons, a Wells

Towns & sites: Yuma, Yuma Crossing State Historic Park, Yuma Territorial Prison State Historic Park, Imperial Dam and National Wildlife Refuge, Palm Canyon, and Kofa National Wildlife Refuge.

Overview: This tour serves up sites in Yuma associated with the history of the American Southwest, refuge areas where you can view wildlife, and an area where you can hike and spot bighorn sheep, if you have the patience.

Routes & mileage: About 270 miles round trip from Yuma. Take U.S. Route 95 north to turnoffs for Imperial Dam, Imperial National Wildlife Refuge, and Palm Canyon.

Time to allow: Two days.

(OPPOSITE PAGE) *Taylor Lake attracts birds and animals to the Imperial National Wildlife Refuge.* MICHAEL COLLIER
(TOP) *The lower Colorado River is an excellent place to see many types of birds, like these American white pelicans.* PETER ENSENBERGER
(ABOVE) *Sunlight barely illuminates a cell at the Yuma Territorial Prison, now a tourist attraction.* JEFF KIDA

Fargo freight wagon, a fire hose cart, a buckboard and a sulky, a baggage cart from the Southern Pacific Railroad, a pilot wheel from the steamboat *Mohave,* and a 1931 Ford Model A Truck used by people fleeing the Depression Era drought and heading for California.

The first steamboats, I learn, were big side-wheelers, like the *Uncle Sam.* But over time, the shallow-draft stern-wheelers, which could navigate in less than three feet of water, proved more practical. Carrying up to 50 tons of cargo, big boats like the *Colorado, Cocopah,* and *Explorer* could make the 240-mile round trip from Port Isabel on the Gulf of California to the Yuma Crossing in four to five days. Gross profit for such a trip was estimated at $4,000, an enormous sum in the 1860s.

In another building, I discover a diorama, created by high school American history students, showing the location of the buildings of the original quartermaster depot. The grounds are shown buzzing with activity. At river's edge, miniature stevedores unload a steamboat's cargo onto freight wagons hauled by mule teams.

Heading back toward the park's visitors center, I look across the river to St. Thomas Mission, formerly Fort Yuma, overlooking the river. When the fort was abandoned by the military, it was transferred to the Quechan Indian Tribe, which now houses a museum and tribal headquarters on the site.

At the visitors center, I survey an exhibit of the Old Plank Road, that for a period of 10 years in the early 1900s enabled travelers to drive automobiles across the Algodones Dunes west of Yuma.

The Old Plank Road exhibit reminds me of movie stills I had seen the day before at the Century House Museum in Yuma's downtown historic district. The stills illustrate dozens of motion pictures filmed on location in the Yuma sand dunes, particularly those requiring desert scenes. In chronological order, a very short list of some

(ABOVE) *Yuma's historic north end includes the Colorado River, Quartermaster Depot, and Yuma Crossing State Historical Park.* RICHARD EMBERY
(BELOW, LEFT) *The wind whips the sand dunes just east of Yuma into mounds and wrinkles.* ROBERT G. McDONALD
(RIGHT) *The Colorado River winds through the Imperial Wildlife Refuge on its way to Yuma.* MICHAEL COLLIER

of my favorites includes *The Big Trail*, 1930; *The Barbarian*, 1933; *Suez*, 1933; *The Lost Patrol*, 1934; *Beau Geste*, 1939; *The Road to Morocco*, 1942; *Sahara*, 1943; *The Desert Fox* (a big favorite), 1951; *The Badlanders*, 1958; *Seven Days in May*, 1964; and *Flight of the Phoenix*, 1966.

Early the next morning, I enter the Yuma Territorial Prison State Historic Park. With its looming guard tower, the Snake Pit where incorrigibles were chained, and tiered bunks in dank cells where convicts slept on straw mattresses infested with bedbugs, the prison appears dreadful to the modern eye. And in the years since its closing in 1909, lurid newspaper accounts of prison life, pulp fiction, and movies, such as *The Badlanders*, have earned the Territorial Prison an unwarranted reputation as an unimaginably cruel hellhole.

In touring the museum and prison grounds, however, I learn that in its day the Yuma Territorial Prison was considered exemplary for its humane treatment of prisoners. The prison was lighted by electricity. Schooling, medical care, and a library were available to prisoners, and items crafted by inmates in their spare time were offered at weekend craft shows. Some of these are still displayed in the prison museum. Local citizens scoffed at these amenities and wrote letters to the newspaper, scolding prison officials for pampering the inmates.

But life for prisoners, male and female, was no picnic. Stiflingly hot in summer, the prison was often overcrowded, meals were heavy on bacon and beans, and disease was rampant. Of the 3,069 convicts confined at Yuma through the years, 111 died there. Tuberculosis alone killed 45 inmates. Among other causes of death were suicide and the being shot by prison guards while trying to

escape. On a hillside above the prison, a humble cemetery contains the unmarked graves of dead convicts.

Before becoming a city museum and then a state park in 1961, Yuma Territorial Prison buildings were used briefly as classrooms for Yuma Union High School students. During the Great Depression of the late 1920s and 1930s, prison cells sheltered hoboes and homeless families.

Driving north from Yuma on U.S. Route 95, I pass vast fields of ripening vegetables, reminding me that Yuma is not only a resort city whose permanent population of 65,000 swells to more than 150,000 with the arrival of winter visitors or "snowbirds" from the northern United States and Canada. Yuma is also the wintertime vegetable capital of the American West. Varieties of lettuce, broccoli, cauliflower, cabbages, leeks, endive, asparagus, lemons, peaches, and pecans — as many as three plantings annually for some crops — are harvested in the Yuma area's fertile valleys. Irrigation water is diverted from the Colorado River, which in times past layered the river valleys with rich sediments. Labor for planting and transplanting, hoeing and thinning, harvesting and packing, comes from Mexico. Daily, in peak season, more than 20,000 workers cross at San Luis, a border town south of Yuma, to be transported to the fields in brightly colored school buses.

About 20 miles north of Yuma, I turn west off of U.S. Route 95 and drive about five miles to Imperial Dam, which not only diverts Colorado River water into canals that irrigate California's productive Imperial Valley, but also creates a vast Arizona reservoir known as the Imperial National Wildlife Refuge. The dam site is a favorite stop for admirers of grand feats of engineering, while the refuge is a popular spot for wildlife viewing. The route to the

Imperial Refuge visitors center is on the Martinez Lake Road, which turns west off of U.S. Route 95 approximately three miles north of the Imperial Dam Road.

I have visited the refuge during every season of the year. My fondest recollection is of a kayak excursion in the dead of winter from Blythe, California, downstream to Martinez Lake. In five days on the river, I saw only one other boat, a small, five-horsepower hunter's skiff, heading in the opposite direction. Along the way, I saw bald eagles congregated on sand bars, snowy egrets, Canada geese, bank beavers, great blue herons, coyotes, wild burros and mustangs, mallards, white pelicans, cormorants, herons, kingfishers, ducks, and coots.

For those who like a faster pace than that of a self-propelled boat, the time to be on the Colorado River with power watercraft is spring through fall when the water is warm and the river teems with skiers and other recreationists. After September, the weather stays mild, but the river is colder.

Back on U.S. 95, I drive north approximately 40 miles to a road that turns east toward Palm Canyon in the Kofa National Wildlife Refuge. Initially, the road crosses "desert pavement," uniformly sized stones so closely packed on flat terrain that they resemble blacktop. The flats are covered by creosote bush, a long-lived shrub that tolerates extreme heat and drought. Little else grows here.

(BELOW) *The lower Colorado River, with flat water and ample fish cover, attracts anglers.* JAMES TALLON
(RIGHT) *Palm Canyon lies in the heart of the Kofa (short for King of Arizona) Mountains.* DAVID LAZAROFF
(OPPOSITE PAGE) *The Kofas provide an ideal habitat for desert bighorn sheep.* PETER ENSENBERGER

As the road climbs, I begin to see a few saguaro cactuses, varieties of cholla cactus, and foothills paloverde trees. Large chunks of volcanic rubble litter the roadside and cinder cones. In spring, brittlebush, globemallow, ocotillo, and Mexican poppies bloom by the road. When it is well watered by late spring rains, vegetation bordering the track is lush.

Hiking into Palm Canyon, I round a corner to encounter, face to face, a desert bighorn ram. As astonished to see me as I am him, he stares, muscles twitching, then bounds upslope at incredible speed. I climb up narrow Palm Canyon toward a group of wild palms I had glimpsed growing in a cleft. After an hour of strenuous climbing, I crawl through a keyhole in the rock and stand before a grove of wild palms, perhaps 40 in all.

They're California fan palms, *Washingtonia filifera*. Botanists believe the trees to be relics of a time when southwestern Arizona was a cooler, wetter place. As the climate dried and heated up, the palms retreated into these canyon niches where they could be sheltered from the fierce midday sun and watered by run-off trickling from the heights.

Very slender and shorter than their domesticated cousins adorning our city boulevards, these wild palms wear last year's untrimmed fronds in shaggy petticoats around their trunks. A fire raced upslope here more than 40 years ago, as you can see from the charred trunks of some of the palms.

Both the Kofa Mountains and the Castle Dome Mountains comprise the Kofa National Wildlife Refuge. Not very high by Arizona standards, these two ranges are extremely rugged, providing ideal habitat for desert bighorn sheep. Although I consider myself something of a desert rat, I hike in these mountains only during cooler months. ♥

When You Go

Century House Museum: 240 South Madison Avenue, Yuma. (520) 782-1841. No charge. Open Tuesday through Saturday, 10 A.M. to 4 P.M.

Imperial National Wildlife Refuge: 40 miles north of Yuma off U.S. Route 95. (520) 783-3371.

Kofa National Wildlife Refuge: Visitors center at 356 West First Street, Yuma. (520) 783-7861. Visitors center is open 7:30 A.M. to 4 P.M., weekdays; from November 15 to March 31, also open weekends, 9 A.M. to 4 P.M.

Martinez Lake: North on U.S. Route 95 about 22 miles north of Yuma. Turn left onto Martinez Lake Road. When the road forks after about 10 miles, the right fork heads to Martinez Lake Marina. Left fork leads to Fisher's Landing. Both marinas offer showers, rest rooms, fuel, boat rental, boat launching, restaurant, groceries. No entry fee. (520) 783-9589 or (800) 876-7004.

Yuma Convention & Visitors Bureau: Receiving on average only 2.94 inches of rain annually, Yuma's weather is warm and dry throughout much of the year, October through April being the peak travel season. City maps available for a fee. (520) 783-0071.

Yuma County Chamber of Commerce: (520) 782-2567.

Yuma Crossing State Historic Park: 201 North Fourth Avenue. (520) 329-0471. Admission fee.

Yuma Parks & Recreation: 1793 South First Avenue. For informa-

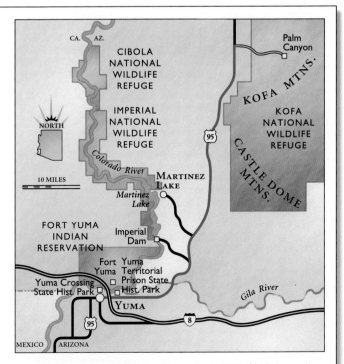

tion on tennis courts, walking and running tracks, softball diamonds, volleyball courts, swimming pools, and more, call (520) 783-1284.

Yuma Territorial Prison State Historic Park: 1 Prison Hill Road. (520) 783-4771. Admission fee.

Roaming Along the Colorado River

AN ECLECTIC MIX OF ATTRACTIONS

by Tom Dollar

It was summer the first time I drove through Quartzsite, situated at the intersection of Interstate 10 and U.S. 95.

"Sleepy little crossroads town," I thought. And, for much of the year, Quartzsite, permanent population hovering around 2,500, is just that. But when the snow flies and temperatures plummet in other parts of the continent, trailers and motor homes begin to occupy Quartzsite's RV parks. When the RV parks overflow, temporary communities of winter visitors sprout on the outlying desert flats. And Quartzsite's population swells.

Visitors love Quartzsite for the mild, sunny days of its low-elevation winter climate, but among the thousands who pour into the area are the many rock hounds and gem and mineral enthusiasts who come for the big February event that really puts the town on the map — the annual Quartzsite Pow Wow, a gem and mineral show. Then, more than a million visitors from all over the world — buyers, sellers, traders, and gawkers — flock to flea markets and exhibition booths set up all over town. Entertainment, cookouts, dancing — for a few days little Quartzsite is one of most bustling destinations in all of Arizona.

On a subsequent pass through Quartzsite on State 95, I was heading for Parker but detoured west on Interstate 10 to Blythe, California, to the site of the Great Blythe Intaglios, giant figures engraved in the earth. Unknown for many years, these enormous etchings were first seen from the air some 50 years ago. One is clearly a human effigy. Arms wide, it measures 160 feet from outspread fingertip to fingertip and 170 feet from head to toe. Another seems to be a horse, but the area's Mohave Indians say it may be a mountain lion. One interpretation of the human figure is that it represents Ha-ak, a child-eating monster of Mohave mythology who was killed by a warrior hero.

Returning to Quartzsite, I drove north on State 95 along the eastern edge of the 278,000-acre Colorado River Indian Reservation, which stretches for about 50 miles on both sides of the Colorado River. Once home only to river tribes, the reservation now houses not only indigenous Mohave and Chemehuevi, but also Navajo and Hopi, an arrangement brought about by a post-World War II Bureau of Indian Affairs mandate.

Just two miles south of Parker is the Colorado Indian Tribes Library and Museum. The museum, dedicated to the more than 10,000 years of Colorado River Indian culture, contains an outstanding collection of Chemehuevi baskets. Known for extremely tight weaving, these baskets are exquisitely woven of such traditional native materials

Towns & sites: Quartzsite, Great Blythe Intaglios, Colorado River Indian Reservation, Parker, the Colorado River, Parker Dam and Lake Havasu, the Havasu National Wildlife Refuge, Bill Williams River, Lake Havasu City and the London Bridge, Alamo Lake State Park, Buckskin Mountain State Park, Cattail Cove State Park, Lake Havasu State Park, and the ghost town of Swansea.

Overview: Here's an eclectic tour touching on a rockhounding capital, ancient intaglios, an Indian reservation and museum, wildlife refuges, river and lake activities, and a ghost town.

Routes & mileage: 75 miles from Quartzsite to Lake Havasu City via State Route 95. A side trip to Blythe, California, via Interstate 10 and U.S. Route 95 adds about 50 miles.

Time to allow: Two days.

(OPPOSITE PAGE) *Just before flowing into the Colorado River, the Bill Williams River provides ideal habitat for the Havasu National Wildlife Refuge.* GEORGE H.H. HUEY
(TOP) *Alamo Lake State Park on the Bill Williams River appeals to anglers and nature lovers.* LES MANEVITZ
(ABOVE) *Rock hounds and mineral enthusiasts flock to Quartzsite and mild weather every February.* BILL SPERRY

as willow and devil's claw. Among other craft items, the museum also features beadwork, dolls, cradle boards, pottery, silverwork, Hopi kachinas, and overlay jewelry.

Like most communities located along Arizona's "West Coast" on the lower Colorado River, Parker is big on water recreation throughout the year, but especially in spring (which arrives early here), early summer, and fall. An event popular among cycling enthusiasts is the February "Another Dam Race and Ride," a professional bicycle race so-named for a portion of its route across the Parker Dam roadway.

Featuring a parade, street dance, and balloon rides, the Lions Club Balloonfest fills the March sky with colorful hot-air balloons. Also scheduled for March are the La Paz County Fair and the Water Ski Marathon. May brings the Parker Enduro Speedboat Race. Billed as the "granddaddy of powerboat racing," it is held at Bluewater Marina north of town. But the event that may attract more participants and onlookers than any other is the Annual Innertube River Float, which meanders five miles down the Colorado River from Patria Flats to Blue Water Marina. In June, an innertube float attracts more than 600 entrants of all ages from both the California and Arizona sides of the river. Registrants get a free T-shirt, and although most tubers are in it for the fun and games, some do race to the finish. Prizes are awarded for first place, largest group, oldest and youngest tuber, and best inner tube float. The Innertube River Float kicks off summer activities on the river.

Leaving Parker, I drive north on State 95 about 16 miles to Parker Dam, the world's deepest, which sits on solid rock 235 feet below the Colorado's riverbed. I climb to a scenic overlook to get a view of Lake Havasu, the 45-mile-long reservoir behind the dam, where fishing boats bob lightly on the calm waters. A few miles north of the dam, the Bill Williams River flows under the State 95 bridge into Lake Havasu.

As you drive north across the bridge, the Havasu National Wildlife Refuge is on your left and the Bill Williams Unit of the Havasu Refuge is on your right. Established in 1941, the refuge features varied terrain of rugged desert uplands, riparian habitat, and a marshy cattail delta at the confluence. The refuge was set aside to provide habitat for waterfowl, and, true to its purpose, the refuge attracts many species, including herons, egrets, grebes, mallards, northern pintails, and wintering Canada geese. Also found on the refuge are threatened or endangered species, such as the willow flycatcher and the Yuma clapper rail. Other wildlife in the refuge include muskrat, beaver, mule deer, javelina, bighorn sheep, several species of raptors including bald eagles, and a variety of amphibians and lizards.

Although much of it was washed out by flooding in 1993, a gravel road turns off State 95 into the Bill Williams River Refuge south of the bridge. The road is still passable

(ABOVE) *The nearly 20,000-acre Lake Havasu provides a variety of recreational activities, such as boating, fishing, skiing, and tours.* KERRICK JAMES
(OPPOSITE PAGE) *The lights of London Bridge, brought in the 1970s to Lake Havasu City, reflect in the placid water below just before dawn.* RANDY PRENTICE

for roughly three miles. Hikers are invited to park at the gate barring the road and explore the area on foot.

How does an erstwhile fishing camp with urban ambitions become one of the fastest-growing cities in Arizona and a top tourist attraction to boot? Easy. The town's founding father, whose make-up is equal parts inventor, industrialist, and entrepreneur, buys the famed London Bridge at auction, catalogs and numbers each block while dismantling it, and rebuilds the span in downtown Lake Havasu City. Preposterous, you say? But that's exactly what happened.

Lake Havasu City's story is really that of Robert P. McCulloch Sr., the chain saw manufacturer who moved his operation from California to the Lake Havasu site in the 1960s. McCulloch's idea was that a good-sized master-planned community would develop around his manufacturing plant. Largely owing to the ups and downs of the chain-saw business, however, it never happened. And eventually McCulloch moved his factory to Tucson.

Then London Bridge, which had arched over the River Thames for 136 years, entered the picture. McCulloch and business partner C.V. Wood were watching television, the story goes, when it was announced that 33,000 tons of granite stone from the London Bridge were for sale. In a moment of uncanny inspiration and foresight, the partners agreed to buy it on the spot. If the chainsaw business wasn't the key to municipal growth, maybe the London Bridge was. So he bought it, tore it down, and spent more than $7 million shipping it across the Atlantic Ocean, through the Panama Canal to Long Beach, California, then overland to Lake Havasu City where 10,276 pieces of this fantastic jigsaw puzzle were reassembled over four years. Finally, the last stone was put in place and the bridge was dedicated in 1971. When it was finished, water was diverted from Lake Havasu to a man-made channel beneath the bridge.

It worked. Today, true to fantasy axiom "If you build it, they will come," some 1.5 million tourists annually flock to Lake Havasu to see the bridge. Pubs and shops with a decidedly British flavor crowd malls at either end of the bridge. Resorts and motels sprouted to accommodate visitors. And as a tourist attraction that pumps some $35 million into the local economy, London Bridge created jobs for Lake Havasu denizens, which today number more than 32,000, making the city, incorporated in 1978, the largest in Mohave County.

But the bridge isn't the whole story in Lake Havasu City. Fishing is good, and water sports are terrific. Modern tennis and racquetball courts are available, as well as three 18-hole golf courses. Boat tours leave regularly from docks beneath the bridge.

One of my favorite tours runs from the bridge all the way up to Topock Gorge, an unspoiled portion of Havasu Wildlife Refuge where majestic rock outcroppings called the Needles provide scenic thrills, and waterfowl abound. The tour also visits an Indian rock art site. Four-wheel-drive eco-adventure tours into the desert country around Lake Havasu are also available. Canoe rentals can be arranged at Topock where Interstate 40 crosses into California. An information center near the bridge provides details on the tours, rentals, and other aspects of the lake.

Each month in Lake Havasu City features a festival of one kind or another. For young and old alike an end-of-year highlight is the December boat parade under the lighted London Bridge. Other festivities include the Polar Bear Ski Run and the Dixieland Jazz Fest in January, the February Red Man Bass Tournament, and the Annual Special Olympics Spring Games in March. Lake Havasu is a fisherman's mecca and, in addition to the Red Man Tournament, several events throughout the year celebrate the area's good fishing.

Campers, fishing enthusiasts, boaters, and water skiers should not overlook four excellent Arizona state parks in the area. The first can be reached by driving east from Quartzsite on Interstate 10 to Exit 31, the interstate's link with U.S. Route 60. Drive about 29 miles northeast on U.S. 60 to Wenden, then 38 miles north on the paved road to Alamo Lake State Park. The park lies along a flood-control reservoir behind the Alamo Dam on the Bill Williams River between the Rawhide and Buckskin mountain ranges. Wild burros roam the area, along with desert bighorn sheep and, in winter, bald eagles fish the reservoir. Boat rentals are available at a well-stocked marina store.

The second park, approximately 11 miles north of Parker just off State 95, is the Buckskin Mountain State Park. With the Buckskin Mountains on one side and the Colorado River on the other, the park is ideally situated for hikers, fishermen, water-sports enthusiasts, and nature lovers. Hikers heading into the Buckskins sometimes encounter desert bighorn sheep. River Island, a

(BELOW) *Tour boats make a run to rock formations known as the Needles in remote Topock Gorge.* JERRY JACKA (OPPOSITE PAGE) *Buckskin Mountain State Park, near Parker Dam, provides access to the Colorado River, camping, and scenic overviews.* LES MANEVITZ

The fourth is Lake Havasu State Park (Windsor Beach), a metropolitan park located north of London Bridge just off London Bridge Road. Popular among swimmers as a day-use area, the park also offers boat launching and camping.

Finally, while you are in the area, consider taking a side trip to the ghost town of Swansea, which lies approximately 23 miles east of Parker via paved and graded dirt roads. The ghost town is on land administered by the Bureau of Land Management. Concerned about the preservation of the old mining town's remnants, the agency has posted signs warning against the removal or destruction of antiquities.

The town was named for the birthplace of George Mitchell, a native of Swansea, Wales. In 1907, Mitchell invested in the Clara Gold and Copper Mining Company, which held claims in the area. The mining operation and the town survived until 1937, a fairly lengthy duration in the annals of Arizona mining operations.

In its heyday, Swansea boasted 500 mostly male residents, a post office, saloons (of course), a general store, Mitchell's own two-story house, a group of wood-frame buildings, and a moving picture show. There was even a mining camp newspaper, the *Swansea Times*, an unofficial mayor, and an insurance salesman, whose services, given the perilous nature of mining activity, were most certainly required. ⚑

unit of the Buckskin Mountain State Park, is located just north off State 95.

The third park — Cattail Cove State Park — lies 15 miles south of Lake Havasu City just off of State 95. Cattail Cove is unique among state parks in that it offers 125 boat-access-only campsites along the Arizona shore of Lake Havasu in addition to a modern campground within the park proper. Cattail Cove is a favorite among year-round water recreationists.

When You Go

About Route 95: Be aware that between Yuma and Quartzsite, 95 is a U.S. highway. At Quartzsite, the U.S. highway goes west, coinciding with Interstate 10, into California and then north along the Colorado River. Between Quartzsite and Bullhead City, Arizona, 95 is a state road.

Alamo Lake State Park: (520) 669-2088.

Bill Williams River area: U.S. Fish and Wildlife Service refuge office, Parker. (520) 667-4144.

Buckskin Mountain State Park: (520) 667-3231.

Cattail Cove State Park: (520) 855-1223.

Lake Havasu State Park: (520) 855-2784.

Lake Havasu Tourism Bureau: 314 London Bridge Road, Lake Havasu City. (800) 2-HAVASU or (520) 453-3444.

Parker Area Chamber of Commerce: (520) 669-2174.

Additional park information: For additional information on state parks, call the Arizona State Parks offices, Monday through Friday, 8 A.M. to 5 P.M., (602) 542-4174. On the Internet, visit www.pr.state.az.us/

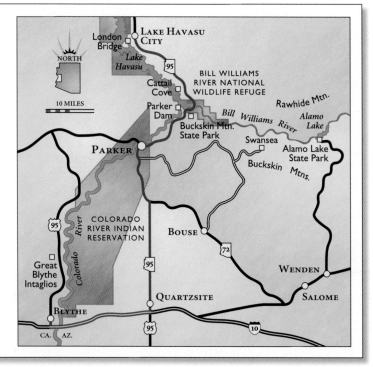

Where the Old West Meets the Water

HISTORIC ROUTE 66 AND LAKE MEAD

by Tom Dollar

Arriving in Kingman, the first thing I do is drive southeast of town to Hualapai Mountain Park. I want an impression of the lay of the land around Kingman, and Hualapai Mountain seems a good place to start.

The mountain is named for the Hualapai Indians, whose name translates to "pine tree people." Sure enough, 10 miles up the winding mountain road I pass through stands of piñon and juniper and into ponderosa pine and oak. Turning off the air conditioning, I roll down my windows to let in the cool, pine-scented air.

Atop the mountain I discover some old, stone rental cabins, a picnic ground, recreational facilities, and hiking trails. With binoculars I scan Hualapai Peak, which tops out at 8,417 feet, and Hayden and Aspen Peaks, both in the 8,000-foot range. Way up, on the north-facing slopes, I'm surprised to see aspen and Douglas fir trees. But like all lofty mountains surrounded by flat, arid terrain, Hualapai Mountain is called a sky island in the desert.

Coming down, I park at an overlook and scan the valley nestling Kingman, the seat of Mohave County, in a pass between the Cerbat and Hualapai mountains. Historic Route 66, the "Mother Road" across America, runs through Kingman's downtown district. Celebrated in song lyrics as one of many towns along the famous highway ("Kingman, Barstow, San Bernardino"), Kingman used to be a town motorists had to pass through. Nowadays, speeding on Interstate 40, you could bypass Kingman, but that would be a mistake.

The National Register of Historic Buildings lists 62 sites in Kingman. One of them, the Hotel Brunswick, was built in 1909. The restored Brunswick is now a bed-and-breakfast establishment. Its dining room looks out on Andy Devine Avenue, named for the late movie actor, a Kingman native son who grew up right next door in the Beale Hotel, managed by his parents.

My next top is the Powerhouse visitors center, perhaps the oldest reinforced concrete structure in Arizona. Once an actual powerhouse operated by the Desert

Towns & sites: Kingman, Hualapai Mountain Park, Historic Route 66, Oatman, Bullhead City, Chloride, Temple Bar, Hoover Dam, and Lake Mead National Recreation Area.

Overview: Two legs of this tour use Kingman as a hub. On one, you venture over Historic Route 66 to the old mining town of Oatman, where burros roam the streets, and then to Bullhead City on the Colorado River. On the second, your destination is Hoover Dam and the Lake Mead National Recreation Area, with stops at another old mining town and a resort-water sports center on Lake Mead.

Routes & mileage: Round trip, Kingman-Oatman-Bullhead City-Kingman, about 90 miles via Historic Route 66, a local road, State Route 95 and State Route 68. Kingman to Hoover Dam via State Route 93, with side trips to Chloride and Temple Bar via local roads, 145 miles.

Time to allow: Three or four days.

(LEFT) *Desert vegetation dominates the lower part of Hualapai Mountain Park.* DAVID H. SMITH

(ABOVE, RIGHT) *Colors and shapes formed by a setting sun and clouds in the Cerbat Mountains bear a resemblance to Arizona's state flag.* GEORGE STOCKING

(RIGHT) *Diners enjoy the ambience at the Hualapai Mountain Lodge.* DAVID H. SMITH

Power and Water Company, the renovated 90-year-old building now houses a tourist center operated by the Kingman Chamber of Commerce; the Carlos Elmer Memorial Gallery, which displays color photographs of another Kingman native, the late Carlos Elmer, a long-time contributor to *Arizona Highways;* and the Historic Route 66 Association.

Kingman's name was bestowed by railroader Lewis Kingman, and railroad development and Kingman history are intertwined. The transcontinental rail line laid down by the Atlantic and Pacific Railroad (now the Santa Fe) cuts through Kingman, and the town celebrates its railroad history with exhibits in its museums and parks. Inside the Powerhouse, a model train goes round and round on tracks at mezzanine level while tooting its tiny whistle. Also occupying the Powerhouse is a soda fountain and deli bar, a shop replete with just about anything a model railroad buff could desire, and the Route 66 Museum, which features photos, murals, and dioramas that detail the history of the famous highway in Arizona.

I obtain a map at the visitors center and spend the afternoon walking Kingman's historic district, including a visit to the Mohave Museum of History and Art, Locomotive Park, and the Bonelli House, one of a number of buildings constructed of locally quarried tufa stone. Presented to the city by the Santa Fe Railroad, Steam Engine No. 3759 stands in Locomotive Park. And, as one might expect, the Mohave Museum accents Kingman's past: ranching, mining, railroad development, Route 66, and, of course, the town's favorite son, Andy 'Jingles' Devine.

The following morning finds me driving west from Kingman on Historic Route 66, the erstwhile Main Street of America. I'm heading for Oatman, a defunct gold-mining town that in its heyday, 1904 through 1931, produced $36 million in ore.

Out of Kingman, Route 66 moves gently across the Sacramento Valley until it reaches the Black Mountain foothills, where it rises abruptly, winding through the rugged hills and around curves with steep drops. In the 1930s, many travelers were daunted by this portion of the route, and local citizens earned extra cash by chauffeuring westward migrants across the Black Mountains. Later, the highway was moved south across flatter terrain.

As I maneuver the sheer switchbacks up toward Oatman, I spot a small herd of burros grazing on a hillside and pull over to watch them. These feral burros are descendants of prospectors' pack animals released into the wild when gold ore petered out. There are more of them here in the Black Mountains than anywhere else in Arizona.

Also, I keep an eye out for bighorn sheep, which also thrive in these hills.

Named for a pioneering family killed by Indians near Gila Bend, Oatman's peak population was 10,000 in the

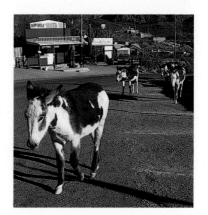

days when 50 mines operated in the district. For westbound travelers in the 1930s, the town was a last, cool stop before crossing the Colorado River into California's broiling Mohave Desert.

Today, Oatman is a quaint tourist attraction known for

its arts and crafts shops, re-enactments of Old West gunfights, and the wild burros that roam its streets. The burros, which inspired the town to inaugurate the International Burro-Biscuit Throwing Contest, wander in from the desert every morning to be pampered and fed by tourists. At sundown they leave.

I leave before sundown, bound for Bullhead City on the Colorado River. The air grows warmer and the terrain flatter as I descend toward the river. Unlike people in Kingman and Oatman, no one in Bullhead City wears Western garb. Instead, I observe lots of baggy shorts, oversized T-shirts, and flip-flop sandals. A lot of folks are bronzed and sport hair a trifle sun bleached from hours spent jet-skiing, boating, fishing, water-skiing, or swimming.

Incorporated in 1984 with a population of barely 5,000, Bullhead City now boasts a population of nearly 30,000 and takes pride in its status as a prime destination resort town on Arizona's "West Coast." Warm, sunny days bring boaters and other water sports enthusiasts to the area in droves. And for lovers of nightlife, the gambling casinos of Laughlin, Nevada, are just a short hop across a bridge spanning the Colorado.

Before leaving Bullhead City I stop at the Colorado River Museum on the edge of town. The tiny museum spotlights local history with old photographs, dioramas, and other displays on mining, native Americans, and railroad development. But the one that catches my eye is about steamboats. Because of all the dams along its length, few people think of the Colorado as a steamboat river. But between 1852 and 1877, shallow-draft sternwheelers plied

the Colorado from the Gulf of California north to the mouth of the Virgin River, nearly 600 miles.

Kingman is the hub along whose spokes I explore this section of Western Arizona, so I return there early the next morning, gas up my vehicle, and head north on U.S. 93 toward Hoover Dam and Lake Mead. But I've got a couple of side trips to make along the way.

About 15 miles north of Kingman, I turn right (east) and drive four miles to Chloride. Founded in 1862 when its post office, the oldest still operating in the state, was established, Chloride was a mining town in the Cerbat Mountain foothills. Seventy-five gold, silver, lead, zinc, and copper mines were active in the area at its peak, and the town's population exceeded 2,000. Now, the 300 people who live here are mix of retirees, artists and artisans, musicians, and others who simply enjoy life off the beaten path.

Driving in, I note that many of the old buildings are occupied by antique and gift shops and that other establishments include a couple of saloons, a grocery store, a few cafes, and a bed and breakfast inn. At the visitors center, a friendly woman named Jeannie offers me a map

(OPPOSITE PAGE, ABOVE) *The Black Mountains, in which is nestled the old mining town of Oatman along Historic Route 66 southwest of Kingman, were called the Sierra de Santiago, or St. James Range, by a Spanish explorer.* JERRY JACKA
(OPPOSITE PAGE, BELOW) *Wild burros roam Oatman braying for food handouts.* JAMES TALLON
(ABOVE) *An aged gas pump decorates a roadside in off-the-beaten path Chloride.*
(LEFT) *Now worn out, the Cerbat Mountains once bore enough gold and other ores to sustain 75 mines.* BOTH BY GEORGE STOCKING

on which she pinpoints some of the town's attractions, such as the old jail, train station, bank, and saloon.

She also directs me to a site on a dirt road about a mile from town where I'll find some rock art. Some of the petroglyphs are suspect, likely scratched on the rocks by kids at play, but the bighorn sheep figure and the man in the maze appear authentic.

(ABOVE) *Boats of all types find harbor at Boulder Beach Marina in the Lake Mead National Recreation Area.*
LAURENCE PARENT
(BELOW) *Dramatic rock formations, such as Napoleon's Tomb, form landmarks in upper Lake Mead.*
(OPPOSITE PAGE) *Hoover Dam rises 726 feet above the Colorado River.* BOTH BY NICK BEREZENKO

On enormous rocks opposite the petroglyphs are grand-scale "murals" created in the mid-1960s by a miner named Roy Purcell. One painting depicts Chloride in boom times; another appears to represent its demise. Others imitate Indian art — animals, human figures, suns, and moons. After he left Chloride, Purcell became famous. Now, his art works are owned by major corporations as well as private collectors.

Back on U.S. 93, I drive 34 miles before taking the turnoff to the right for Temple Bar. Named for a nearby rock formation shaped like a temple, Temple Bar originally was a mining camp at the mouth of the Virgin River.

When Hoover Dam backed up the waters of the Colorado River to create Lake Mead, the largest man-made lake in the United States, Temple Bar became a boat landing, lake resort, and campground managed by the National Park Service as part of the Lake Mead National Recreation Area. The first national recreation area in the United States, the Lake Mead National Recreation Area includes both Lake Mead and Lake Mohave, which lies downstream from Hoover Dam.

On the road to Temple Bar, I pass a couple of trailers transporting fishing boats to the landing and another going the opposite way hauling a ski boat. In summer, Temple Bar becomes a resort center for swimmers, water-skiers, scuba divers, jet skiers, fishermen, and boaters. Hikers venturing into nearby rocky hills may encounter

desert bighorn sheep, which often come in broad daylight to the shores of Lake Mead to drink.

I camp in the desert near Temple Bar and head out at dawn the next morning for Hoover Dam. Before taking a tour, I browse the new visitors center, which opened in 1995. The center features photographs and interactive displays on geology, dam building, and the area's natural history. Just before the tour begins, I step into the auditorium to watch a short film on the dam's history.

The 726-foot-high Hoover Dam has been called one of world's civil engineering wonders, and it is. The concrete used in the dam would pave a 16-foot-wide, 8-inch-thick strip from San Francisco to New York City. And the dam was the first man-made structure to exceed the masonry mass of the Great Pyramid of Giza.

When I look at old photos and film footage of its construction from 1931 to 1935, I marvel at the ingenuity, courage, and fortitude of the men who built Hoover Dam. In heat that rivals the scorching intensity of Death Valley, men called high-scalers, worked without hard hats and other safety equipment, dangling over the cliff face on thin ropes to jackhammer loose rock and drill holes for blasting charges. In the bottom of Black Canyon, other men waited for gantry cranes to lower enormous buckets of concrete that they shoveled into place and tamped down with rubber-booted feet. Yes, much of Hoover Dam was built by hand, and, amazingly, it was finished two years ahead of schedule. ◪

When You Go

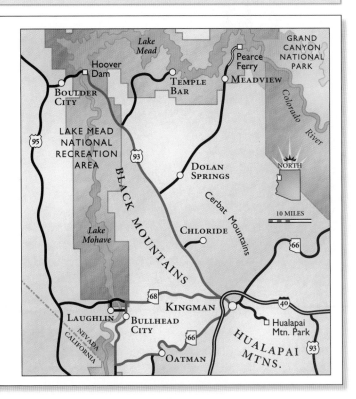

Bullhead Area Chamber of Commerce: (520) 754-4121.

Chloride Chamber of Commerce: (520) 565-2204.

Colorado River Museum: Half mile north of the Laughlin bridge on State 95, Bullhead City. Donations requested. (520) 754-3399.

Historic Route 66 Association of Arizona: In the Powerhouse visitors center. (520) 753-5001. Web site: *www.ctaz.com/~azrt66/*

Hoover Dam: (702) 293-8321. Admission fee. Web site: *www.hooverdam.com/*

Kingman Chamber of Commerce: Powerhouse visitors center, 120 W. Andy Devine Avenue. (520) 753-6106. Web site: *www.ctaz.com/~sueq/kmnonline/kmnonline.html/*

Lake Mead National Recreation Area: General information, (702) 293-8907. Visitors center at Boulder City, Nevada. (702) 293-8990. No charge. Web site: *www.nps.gov/lame/*

Mohave Museum of History and Arts: Quarter mile east of I-40 at 400 W. Beale Street, Kingman. (520) 753-3195. Admission fee.

Oatman events: (520) 768-7400 (Fast Fanny's Gift Shop).

Temple Bar Resort: (520) 767-3211.

A Sonoran Desert Sojourn

IN THE FOOTSTEPS OF EXPEDITIONS

by Sam Negri

When people encounter the surprisingly green desert in the hills and hollows that stretch for 150 miles southwest of Tucson, their reactions vary considerably. Many are awed by the uncluttered landscape and the dense stands of slow-growing giant saguaro cactus, many of which began life when Abraham Lincoln was still a boy. Spanish explorers considered this environment harsh and inhospitable, but the Tohono O'odham people (formerly called Papago) who preceded them, and who still are there today, relate to this desert with religious depth.

This is the Sonoran Desert, an arid landscape of cactus and creosote bush interspersed with volcanic mountains and laced with thickets of mesquite, ironwood, and paloverde trees. It is an intriguing, almost mysterious, terrain of deep arroyos, lichen-covered rocks, and sandy washes where coyotes, rattlesnakes, antelope jackrabbits, and javelina (a wild pig) are common. If winter rains have been plentiful, it's a land that produces a striking array of wildflowers in the spring.

Between Kinney Road on the western edge of Tucson and the Mexican border via State 86 and State 85 — a 145-mile stretch through the Tohono O'odham reservation and Organ Pipe Cactus National Monument — there's not a single traffic light.

To begin this tour, take Interstate 19 south from Interstate 10 in Tucson to the Ajo Way Exit. Turn right (west) at the ramp. Ajo Way becomes State 86 when the road leaves the city at Kinney Road. After about 22 miles, you come to the junction of State 286 at Three Points, also called Robles Junction. State 286 leads south 46 miles to Sasabe on the Mexican border. Stay right at Three Points for this trip.

After you leave Tucson, you can see some 40 miles in the distance the white domes of Kitt Peak National Observatory in the Quinlan Mountains. If you want to visit the observatory and its visitors center, watch on your left for State 386, about 31.5 miles from Kinney Road. From the winding, paved road up the mountain, you can get a commanding view of the countryside. The visitors center and picnic grounds, located on a ridge 6,875 feet above sea level and 4,000 feet above the desert floor, is open to the public daily from 9 A.M. to 4 P.M., except Thanksgiving, Christmas, and New Year's days. Admission is free.

When you reach the road to Kitt Peak, you are on the Tohono O'odham Indian Reservation. The mountain range that accommodates the telescopes is a sacred place to these desert-dwelling people because I'itoi, the central

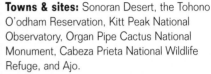

Towns & sites: Sonoran Desert, the Tohono O'odham Reservation, Kitt Peak National Observatory, Organ Pipe Cactus National Monument, Cabeza Prieta National Wildlife Refuge, and Ajo.

Overview: Starting in Tucson, you'll travel through a prime segment of the Sonoran Desert that has attracted adventurers since the 1500s. At Organ Pipe, you can drive to an oasis seeping history and legend as well as life-giving water.

Routes & mileage: About 245 miles, including trips to Kitt Peak, an Indian trading post, Organ Pipe, and Ajo. From Tucson, take State Route 86 to State Route 85 at Why.

Time to allow: One or two days.

(OPPOSITE PAGE) *Sonoran Desert plants like chain cholla, brittlebush, and red owl's clover thrive in the Organ Pipe Cactus National Monument.* JACK DYKINGA
(TOP) *The moon and stars backlight saguaro cactuses in this long-exposure shot at the Cabeza Prieta National Wildlife Refuge.* GEORGE STOCKING
(ABOVE) *The observatory housing the four-meter Mayall telescope stands out at Kitt Peak.* EDWARD McCAIN

figure in the Tohono O'odham creation story, is said to reside in a cave near Baboquivari Peak, some 10 miles south of the telescopes.

The O'odham say the world was created when the darkness rubbed against the water and created First Born. After First Born prepared the Earth for habitation, the sky came down, met the earth, and conceived I'Itoi. It was I'itoi who created people from clay and gave them the gift of the crimson evening, regarded by the O'odham as one of the most beautiful sights in their desert world. The Indians say I'itoi then went about creating various creatures, including the deer, which he made by stuffing a mouse. They say the deer has a white belly because I'itoi stuffed the mouse with too much cotton.

I'itoi told the O'odham to remain in the land where they were and where they continue to be, which is the center of the world to them. In that world I'itoi watches over the Tohono O'odham from his cave.

Sells, the seat of tribal government, is on State 86 about 19 miles west of the Kitt Peak turnoff. The tiny community, though it is the capital of the Tohono O'odham reservation, looks like a frontier town. You can buy food and gas there and are likely to see cows and horses wandering in the streets, oblivious to cars and people.

As you leave Sells, still on State 86, the road gets a little hilly and begins to wind through lush desert and widely scattered corrals made of mesquite branches. Thirty-eight miles beyond Sells, watch on your left for Indian Route 21 that leads about 10 miles south to the tiny village of Pisinimo. At a small trading post there you can purchase Tohono O'odham baskets and other crafts.

From the turnoff to Pisinimo, it is 24.5 miles on State 86 to Why and the junction of State 85. Many people have asked why Why is named Why. One joker responded, "Why not?" The truth is that before the road was re-designed, the highway formed a Y where the settlement is located. Now it looks more like a T. Bearing right at the T will bring you, after 10 miles, into the quaint copper mining town of Ajo (pronounced AH-ho), where there are motels, restaurants, and a museum. The visitors center for the Cabeza Prieta National Wildlife Refuge is also located in Ajo. (The town's name means garlic in Spanish and refers to the wild garlic that was found growing there.)

For Organ Pipe Cactus National Monument, bear left at the T in Why onto State 85 south. In 28 miles you'll arrive at the visitors center for the park named for a unique cactus found only in this area — a cactus that looks like a pipe organ without a keyboard. Tent and recreational vehicle camping spaces are available in the park for a fee. The campground, 1.5 miles from the visitors center, has 208 camp units. Drinking water and rest rooms are available but there are no electrical hookups. Most travelers visit the area between November and April. Winter temperatures average 72° F. during the day and 43° overnight. Summertime temperatures frequently get up to 107°, and it's not unusual for the mercury to climb higher.

There are several hiking trails and drives in the monument, which encompasses 516 square miles of rugged desert bordered by jagged mountain peaks. One of the best drives is the 15-mile trip to Quitobaquito Spring.

Puerto Blanco Drive, an unpaved road that can be bumpy at times, connects State 85 with Quitobaquito and continues on for 20 additional miles to return to State 85 at the border town of Lukeville. The route — you can drive it in a sedan — passes through extremely hot, dry, and rocky terrain with no hint that you will come to live springs, a pond lined with cottonwood trees, swamp-like reeds, and an abundance of birds.

As remarkable as a desert oasis may be, the one at Quitobaquito did nothing for the imagination of a New York botanist named William T. Hornaday, who camped there during a 1908 expedition. In his memoir, *Campfires on Desert and Lava*, Hornaday wrote, "Although Quitovaquita [sic] was entirely quiet and inoffensive, its atmosphere was depressing. It is one of the spots in which I would not like to die, and would hate to live."

Others have not shared Hornaday's opinion. Like just about any reliable watering hole in Arizona, Quitobaquito has a long history of human encounters. Melchior Diaz, a member of the Coronado Expedition of 1540, probably stopped there. The Jesuit missionary Eusebio Kino baptized Indian children near there around 1698 and described Quitobaquito simply as "a good place." The Spaniard Juan Bautista de Anza passed it during the expedition of 1774-1775 en route to locate a passage to California. A man named Andrew Dorsey settled there in 1860 and dug the pond. Ten years later there was a store

(OPPOSITE PAGE, TOP) *Baboquivari Peak is a revered place for the Tohono O'odham.* GEORGE STOCKING
(OPPOSITE PAGE, BOTTOM) *The color and mood created by desert storms often produce drama but little rain for plants like the organ pipe cactus.* JACK DYKINGA
(ABOVE) *Saguaro cactus and paloverde trees often have a symbiotic relationship. The tree shelters the cactus until it is able to fend for itself.* RANDY PRENTICE
(RIGHT) *Quitobaquito Spring nourishes an oasis at Organ Pipe Cactus National Monument.* RANDY PRENTICE

and gold mill at the pond, and native people living a quarter mile away. By the time Hornaday's expedition arrived, three Americans and their Tohono O'odham wives were living at the site.

Most of those who stopped to refresh themselves at Quitobaquito's springs were headed west to the goldfields of California, following a route near the Mexican border that came to be known as *El Camino del Diablo*, the Devil's Highway. Most of that route is now included in the 860,000-acre Cabeza Prieta National Wildlife Refuge.

There is less at Quitobaquito today than there was a hundred years ago. Hardly any clues indicate that this isolated spot once was a fairly active way station for travelers (no buildings remain). The clearest clue that the place was once inhabited is on a hill away from the spot most tourists visit. Walk northward from the pond the equivalent of a block or two and you'll discover a solitary but substantial cement gravestone on a small hill. The grave contains all that remains of one Jose Lorenzo Sestier. The gravestone says he was born in Brest, France, and died at "Quitovaquita" in 1900, when he was 74.

According to research by Wilton Hoy, who was a ranger at Organ Pipe for many years, a man named Mikul Levy had a general store at this spot at the turn of the century. Sestier worked for him as a clerk. When Sestier died, Levy erected the gravestone for him. Historians think Sestier probably traveled through this vast desert

(ABOVE) *Saguaro cactus thrive on the bajadas (slopes) and flat land at the base of mountains such as the Ajo range in Organ Pipe National Monument.* DAVID W. LAZAROFF (OPPOSITE PAGE) *Traditional Tohono O'odham basket weavers use natural materials such as yucca, bear grass, and devil's claw.* JERRY JACKA

during the gold rush days and eventually settled at the outpost that was then known as Quitovaquita.

There is a quiet, some might say eerie, atmosphere about Quitobaquito that makes even the wildest stories seem plausible. One of those stories involved a Tohono O'odham girl. Hoy, who collected information about Quitobaquito and Organ Pipe for more than 20 years, relates the story in an unpublished manuscript:

"Arturo Quiroz recalls a near-adventure at the pond. One day during a visit to Quitobaquito, Arturo noticed a Papago girl wearing a large gold ring. Upon inquiring as to the source of the gold, she remained typically silent; however, a query to her father resulted in his atypically instructing his daughter to accompany Arturo to a mine. Arturo drove the girl in a wagon southwest; they were to leave the wagon at Cipriano Ortega's well and walk to the mine. As the couple neared the mine, the girl suddenly balked, obviously frightened. No persuasion from Arturo could lead her on to the mine, so they returned to

Quitobaquito. There, the girl told her father that she had seen a devilish apparition with outstretched claws that warned he would destroy her if she went to the mine.

Ghosts notwithstanding, at least once a year many Tohono O'odham return to Organ Pipe.

Every year on the third Saturday in March — a time when the daytime temperature is likely to be in the 70s — the indigenous people come to the Organ Pipe for O'odham Day, a daylong event that gives visitors an opportunity to learn about the traditional practices of the people who have been at home in the Sonoran Desert for thousands of years.

Park rangers say O'odham Day is the most popular day of the year at Organ Pipe. In recent years, the event has attracted around 1,500 visitors. The park's normal entrance fee is waived for the O'odham Day festivities.

On O'odham Day, the Tohono O'odham (literally "desert people") and their cousins, the Sand Papagos, will gather at the park's visitors center for native dances and demonstrations of various crafts, including basket weaving and pottery-making. In the patio area, ramadas are set up with exhibits dealing with the native language, dry land farming, and other aspects of Tohono O'odham culture. You can also watch kids playing an ancient game called *toka*, which looks a little like sort of a dry-land hockey and used to be played only by the tribe's women.

O'odham Day festivities always begin at 10 A.M. and end at 4 P.M. and include performances of traditional dances by children from the village of Topawa and others from the San Lucy District near Gila Bend. If you go, be prepared to dance because, toward the end of their

performance, schoolchildren are likely to pull you out of the audience to join in a circle dance. ◗

When You Go

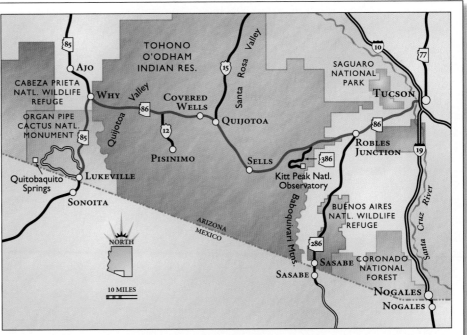

Metropolitan Tucson Convention & Visitors Bureau: (520) 624-1817; (800) 638-8350.

Kitt Peak: For group tours and night tours, call the visitors center, (520) 318-8726, or the recording, (520) 318-8200.

Tohono O'Odham Nation: Call (520) 383-2028 and tell the receptionist what information you are seeking. Baboquivari Mountain Park: (520) 383-2236.

Ajo Chamber of Commerce: (520) 387-7742.

Cabeza Prieta National Wildlife Refuge Visitors Center: On State 85 in Ajo. (520) 387-6483.

Organ Pipe Cactus National Monument Visitors Center: (520) 387-6849.

The Cochise Circle

WHERE FACT AND FOLKLORE MINGLE

by Tom Dollar

Rugged, conifer-clad mountains; broad, grassy valleys; and well-watered canyons — these are the natural features of southeastern Arizona. The territory was once home to the Apache Indian Chiricahua clan, immortalized in place names like Huachuca (meaning "Thunder") Mountain, Geronimo Trail, and Cochise County.

Rich deposits of copper and silver brought boom times to many local settlements during the late 1800s and early 1900s. When ores petered out, many communities became ghost towns, while some, like Tombstone and Bisbee, refashioned themselves as tourist destinations.

Legends of the Old West thrive in southeastern Arizona, where fact and folklore mix to produce stories of lost mines and buried treasures; of the Cochise Stronghold and the gunfight at Tombstone's O.K. Corral; and of vivid characters like Coronado, Geronimo, and Wyatt Earp.

It is a region of great biological diversity and stunning natural beauty, often exquisitely combined in a single location, such as Ramsey Canyon, and the Chiricahua National Monument. But for an uniquely beautiful experience, drive nine miles south of Benson on State Route 90 to the east flank of the Whetstone Mountains and descend into the earth to Kartchner Caverns, Arizona's newest state park. Here our tour begins.

Found in 1974, Kartchner Caverns was not opened to the public until 1999, and then only after park planners were certain that access wouldn't harm its underground environment. Kartchner is a living cave system, meaning that the fantastic, varicolored formations — stalagmites, stalactites, soda straws, helictites, and columns — are still being formed by water slowly seeping through limestone.

Kartchner's pièce de résistance is the Throne Room, an enormous chamber containing a massive floor-to-ceiling, 58-foot column nicknamed Kubla Khan.

From Kartchner Caverns State Park we drop south on State 90 about 10 miles to State 82 and turn east 10 miles to Tombstone, crossing the San Pedro River along the way.

Towns & sites: Benson, Kartchner Caverns State Park, Tombstone, Sierra Vista, Fort Huachuca, Ramsey Canyon, Coronado National Memorial, Bisbee, Douglas, Chiricahua National Monument, Fort Bowie National Historic Site, Sulphur Springs Valley, Cochise Stronghold, Dragoon Mountains, and Willcox.

Overview: We begin with the descent into Kartchner Caverns. By car, we travel along the Cochise Circle to towns and historic sites still bearing the stamp of Apaches, miners, ranchers, and nature's diversity.

Routes & mileage: About 215 miles round trip from Benson. Take Interstate 10 to Benson. Then on to Tombstone via State Route 80; to Sierra Vista and Fort Huachuca via Charleston Road; to Ramsey Canyon, Coronado National Memorial, and Bisbee via State Route 92; to Douglas via State Route 80; to Chiricahua National Monument via State Route 191 and 181; to Willcox via State Route 186.

Time to allow: Two or three days.

(LEFT) *Hedgehog cactus and ponderosa pine trees share southeastern Arizona's Chiricahua Mountains, a part of the Coronado National Forest.* JACK DYKINGA
(ABOVE, RIGHT) *A marker in Boothill Cemetery identifies three victims of Tombstone's famous shoot-out at the O.K. Corral, which occurred in 1881.* RICHARD MAACK
(RIGHT) *The San Pedro River, seen here near Fairbank, provides a riparian habitat in the desert.* RANDY PRENTICE

(FAR LEFT) *The Tombstone Courthouse State Historic Park houses artifacts of Arizona's Wild West days.* (LEFT AND ABOVE) *Actors — these are the Earps — stage the famous Gunfight at the O.K. Corral daily.* ALL BY RICHARD MAACK (OPPOSITE PAGE) *Bisbee thrived first as a copper mining town and currently as an arts and crafts community.* JERRY JACKA

From Tombstone we'll jog a bit southwest to Sierra Vista — again crossing the San Pedro — then south to Bisbee and Douglas. From Douglas, we'll turn north to the Chiricahua National Monument and the Fort Bowie National Historic Site and finally on to Willcox. This 200-plus-mile loop, known as the Cochise Circle, circumscribes a good portion of Cochise County.

Tombstone, "The Town Too Tough To Die," is a prime example of a mining town that boomed, went bust, then boomed again when it remade itself as a tourist attraction.

Silver brought the first boom. In the 1880s, approximately 50 mines operated in the district, and Tombstone's population swelled to 15,000. Plays, operas, and musical revues were performed in the Bird Cage Theater and Schieffelin Hall, named for the town's founder. Twice, the town burned, and twice, it rebuilt. But when subsurface water flooded the mine tunnels, the mines closed, and people left town. Adding insult to injury, officials moved the county seat to Bisbee.

In the 1960s, some Tombstone citizens decided to capitalize on public fascination with the town's Wild West past and that gunfight behind the O.K. Corral in 1881.

Although the details are obscure and still argued over, here's a brief account of the shooting: Bad blood between the Earp brothers and a bunch called the Clanton Gang brings on a series of confrontations that culminate in that now-famous gunfight. Three Clantons are killed, three Earp allies wounded. Later, two of Wyatt's brothers are ambushed — one is killed, the other maimed. Wyatt tracks down those he believes took part in the ambushes and kills them. Then he leaves Tombstone, never to live there again.

This was legendary material, and Tombstone would re-create it. Gunslinging actors would stalk each other. Some of the landmark buildings — such as the Bird Cage Theater, Fly's Photography Gallery, and the Crystal Palace Saloon — would be polished up a bit. Along with the already established Tombstone Courthouse State Historic Park, all this would bring tourists to town. Again, the town would return from the brink of extinction.

Today, Tombstone thrives on its Wild West image. Locals walk the streets in cowboy outfits, Boothill Cemetery attracts scores of visitors, the *Tombstone Epitaph* still publishes, and actors stage the Gunfight at the O.K. Corral daily.

From Tombstone we head south on State 80 then west on State 90 for the San Pedro House, a visitors center operated by the Bureau of Land Management as part of the San Pedro Riparian National Conservation Area, known worldwide for its natural beauty and rich bird-watching. Hiking, camping, horseback riding, and nature study are some other recreational opportunities available along the San Pedro. The San Pedro lures history buffs, too, so at the visitors center pick up trail maps to Murray Springs, where Stone-Age hunters killed bison and mammoths; to Presidio Santa Cruz de Terrenate, a Spanish fort from 1776; and to such mining relics as Fairbank, Charleston, and Grand Central Mill.

Continuing west, we reach Sierra Vista, with its birding events, hot-air balloon rallies, and air shows, and access to hiking, camping, and other activities in the Huachuca Mountains region of the Coronado National Forest.

Established in 1877 for the Apache Wars, Fort Huachuca is the only Arizona cavalry post surviving as a military base. Now a national historic landmark, it retains some of its 19th-century look. The fort's museum documents much of its history — including the service of the brave "Buffalo Soldiers," African-Americans nicknamed by Plains Indians who thought the troopers' curly hair was similar to a buffalo's mane.

Bound for Bisbee on State Route 92, we detour into the Nature Conservancy's 280-acre Ramsey Canyon Preserve. Of southeastern Arizona's numerous, isolated wet canyons, Ramsey is one of the most popular among bird-watchers and nature lovers. Rare lemon lilies grow along the stream, and canyon ponds are home to a species of leopard frog that croaks underwater. In spring, numerous species of hummingbirds migrate here. In autumn, bigtooth maples turn vivid red.

Farther south on State 92 is the turnoff for the Coronado National Memorial. Near here, Francisco Vasquez de Coronado led the first major European expedition into what is now the American Southwest. Just north of the monument is the trailhead for the Crest Trail, which climbs all the way to 9,466-foot Miller Peak in the Huachuca Mountains. Looking south from the memorial, visitors peer across high desert grasslands into Mexico. Ask at the visitors center about going to nearby Montezuma Cave.

Like Tombstone, Bisbee, located in the Mule Mountains, was beset by rough times but managed to survive after copper mining operations ended in the mid-1970s. Bisbee's low-cost housing and mile-high climate attracted painters, sculptors, potters, and writers who helped transform the town into an arts and crafts community. Today, craft shops, galleries, bookstores, coffee bars, and sandwich shops line Tombstone Canyon and Brewery Gulch in the heart of Old Bisbee. The historic Copper Queen Hotel and several bed-and-breakfast inns offer an eclectic experience in lodging.

ment of outlaws while he was sheriff of Cochise County.

Part of the original ranch, now the 2,300-acre San Bernardino National Wildlife Refuge, serves up a habitat of springs, ponds, and grasslands for the benefit of mammals, rare amphibians, and more than 200 bird species.

From Douglas, our loop turns north up State 191 and the Sulphur Springs Valley, then takes State 181 toward the Chiricahua National Monument along the east flank of the Chiricahua Mountains. Millions of years ago a volcanic eruption laid down thousands of feet of volcanic ash that over eons eroded into a stunning array of balanced rocks and weathered spires. This region is called the Heart of Rocks. You can gasp at surreal views from several overlook points and then drive on your way. Or you can hike trails of varying length. Going into the badlands of the Heart of Rocks can take six or seven hours round trip. Other activities available at Chiricahua National Monument include daily tours of the pioneer homestead, Faraway Ranch, and a self-guided nature-trail walk along Bonita Creek.

Driving toward Willcox from Chiricahua National Monument, we turn off State 186 onto a graded road where signs point toward the Fort Bowie National

Taking advantage of Bisbee's unique terrain, which rises steeply from Tombstone Canyon, the community sponsors the annual Bisbee 1,000 or "Great Stair Climb," a run-or-walk race on steps up and down the town's hillsides. Other events, including Brewery Gulch Daze and coaster races down Tombstone Canyon, draw visitors throughout the year.

Many Bisbee visitors tour the closed mines. You can tour the underground Copper Queen Mine by rail car and take van tours of the Lavender open pit mine and Old Bisbee's historic district. Those especially interested in mining should explore Bisbee Mining and Historical Museum's archives and exhibits.

Next stop, Douglas, tucked up against the Arizona-Mexico border. Not a mining town itself, Douglas smelted copper ore from Bisbee's mines. When those closed, Douglas also declined, but the grand Gadsden Hotel, a national historic site, stays open. Businessmen, ranchers, and travelers from both sides of the border still meet in its magnificent, marble-staircased lobby.

East of Douglas 17 miles, out along the Geronimo Trail Road (named 15th Street in town), the Slaughter Ranch, a national historic landmark, also butts up against the Arizona-Mexico border. Originally 65,000 acres extending into Mexico, the ranch was established by John Slaughter, a 5-foot-6-inch former Texas Ranger who became legendary in Arizona for his tough treat-

Historic Site, which commemorates the biggest battle between the U.S. Army and Chiricahua Apaches: The time is July, 1862, during America's Civil War. Most federal troops have been withdrawn from Arizona, and Apaches once again rule the region. Traveling from Tucson to New Mexico, 126 soldiers are ambushed in Apache Pass by 700 Indians. Only their howitzer guns, never before used against Apaches, enable the Army troops to win a 10-hour battle against such overwhelming numbers.

Soon thereafter, Brigadier General James Henry Carleton ordered that Fort Bowie be built in Apache Pass to protect travelers and Apache Springs, the only sure source of good water for miles. The fort closed in 1894, six years after the Apache Wars ended. Today, only a few walls and stone foundations remain, but photos and interpretive signs on the grounds and at the ranger station help re-create the fort's glory days.

Back on State 186, we head to Willcox, a farming and ranching community at the north end of the fertile Sulphur Springs Valley. I've always thought of Willcox as a hub, not only for excursions into the Chiricahua, Dragoon, Pinaleno, and other nearby mountain ranges, but also for visits to the Chiricahua National Monument, Fort Bowie, the Amerind Foundation and Museum, and the Cochise Stronghold. But Willcox rightfully brags about several other things: movie cowboy and native son Rex Allen; its pick-your-own produce farms and orchards; and the Willcox Playa.

Willcox remembers the "singing cowboy" by celebrating Rex Allen Days every fall. A statue of Allen stands in a park across from the Rex Allen Museum. Koko, Allen's famous horse, is buried in the park.

Each January, Willcox throws the Wings Over Willcox Sandhill Crane Celebration, which centers on Willcox Playa. Once a prehistoric lake that measured 200 miles around, the playa is dry most of the year. But when the rains come in July and August, the playa fills to a depth of a few inches. Then, dormant fairy shrimp suddenly hatch and attract water birds that feed on

(LEFT) *The U.S. Army found Cochise Stronghold in the Dragoon Mountains to be impenetrable.* RICHARD MAACK

them. Starting in November, tens of thousands of sand-hill cranes return to roost in the playa over winter.

While in Willcox, if you want to picnic with freshly picked apples or take home vegetables that you harvest, don't pass up the local orchards and fields. The Willcox Chamber of Commerce can tell you what's open to the public and what's in season. Beans and peppers, peaches and pecans, take your pick — literally.

With Willcox, our loop is nearly finished. Visits to two other nearby sites will close the circle.

The first is the Cochise Stronghold in the Dragoon Mountains of the Coronado National Forest. From Willcox, go west on I-10 to Exit 331. Then go south on U.S. 191 for about 12 miles to the marked stronghold turnoff near Sunsites.

In 1860, after a bitter dispute with a young U.S. Army lieutenant, Apache leader Cochise fled with his Chiricahua clan into the Dragoon Mountains, emerging periodically from the natural fortress to battle the Army. In 1872, the Apaches were granted a 55-square-mile reservation here in southeastern Arizona. Two years later, Cochise died; his remains are buried somewhere in the Cochise Stronghold. An excellent campground offering interpretive materials about the Apache people is located at the stronghold on the east side of the Dragoons.

To reach the final stop from the stronghold, take U.S. 191 north to Dragoon Road, turn left, and drive about 10 miles to Dragoon and the Amerind Foundation, a research institute and museum with a gift shop and art gallery. (From I-10 take Exit 318 to Dragoon Road.) Founded in 1937 by philanthropist William Shirley Fulton, Amerind (short for "American Indian") collects and preserves knowledge of the human cultures that occupied this region from prehistory to the present. ◫

When You Go

Amerind Foundation: Admission fee. (520) 586-3666.

Benson-San Pedro Valley Chamber of Commerce: (520) 586-2842.

Bisbee: Chamber of Commerce, (520) 432-5421; toll free, (866) 224-7233. Mining & Historical Museum, (520) 432-7071.

Chiricahua National Monument: Visitors center open daily, 8 A.M. to 5 P.M. Admission fee. (520) 824-3560.

Coronado National Forest: Call Sierra Vista Ranger District in Hereford for information on Cochise Stronghold and other forest sites. (520) 670-4552.

Council Rocks: Rock art site about one hour out of Sierra Vista, north of Tombstone on Forest Service Road 687. Call Douglas Ranger District, (520) 364-3468.

Douglas Chamber of Commerce: (520) 364-2477.

Fort Huachuca Historical Museum: 9 A.M. to 4 P.M., weekdays; 1 P.M. to 4 P.M., weekends. (520) 533-5736.

Kartchner Caverns State Park: 7:30 A.M. to 6 P.M. Closed Christmas. Vehicle fee allows access to Discovery Center, picnic areas, hiking. Cave tours extra. Reservations, (520) 586-2283, 8 A.M. to 5 P.M., weekdays.

Ramsey Canyon: Access limited. For reservations, call (520) 378-2785. Donation requested.

San Bernardino Wildlife Refuge: (520) 364-2104.

San Pedro Riparian National Conservation Area: (520) 458-3559. Closed to vehicles. Call for details.

Sierra Vista Chamber of Commerce/Convention & Visitors Bureau: (520) 458-6940 or (800) 288-3861.

Slaughter Ranch: Open 10 A.M. to 3 P.M., Wednesday through

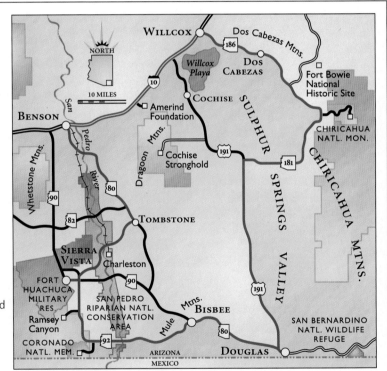

Sunday. Admission fee. (520) 558-2474.

Tombstone Courthouse Historic Park: 8 A.M. to 5 P.M. daily. Admission fee. (520) 457-3311.

Tombstone Chamber of Commerce & Visitors Center: (888) 457-3929. Web site: *www.tombstone.org*

Willcox Chamber of Commerce: (520) 384-2272; (800) 200-2272.

Touring Along Deadmen's Highway

FROM TUCSON TO THE MEXICAN BORDER

by Sam Negri

Interstate 19, which begins at Tucson and ends at Nogales, is an excellent road through the broad valley of the Santa Cruz River. As you travel south, some of the tallest and most accessible mountains in southern Arizona lie east and west of the highway.

The Santa Cruz River bisects the Santa Cruz Valley. Much of southern Arizona bears the stamp of early Spanish explorers in the local architecture and place names. The Santa Cruz River (or "Holy Cross" in Spanish) skirts several mountain ranges whose names reflect this Spanish past. As the river travels downhill from Mexico toward Tucson, it passes near the Patagonia, Atascosa, Cerro Colorado, Tumacacori, Santa Rita, and Santa Catalina mountains. From the 17th century to the present, all of these ranges were explored by Spaniards, Mexicans, and Anglos searching for valuable minerals: gold, silver, lead, zinc, and copper. As you approach Green Valley, some 20 miles south of Tucson on I-19, you'll see enormous pyramid-like excavation mounds to the west where copper mining continues.

In the 19th century, this route was known as Deadmen's Highway (*El Camino de los Muertos*) because Apaches had slaughtered so many in the vicinity. Today, I-19 is a butter-smooth freeway through the tranquil communities of Green Valley, Tubac, and Tumacacori, leading to Nogales, a Mexican border town of intoxicating variety. The distance signs on this road show kilometers instead of miles (multiply kilometers by 0.6 and you'll have miles).

Begin this tour by driving south on I-19 from Exit 260 on I-10. On the outskirts of Tucson, look toward the mountains on your right for a thumbnail view of the alabaster Mission San Xavier del Bac, known locally as the White Dove of the Desert. The mission is on the San Xavier Indian Reservation and was first established in the 1700s. To reach it, take Exit 91, San Xavier Road.

About 22 miles south of the exit for San Xavier, before you come to Green Valley, take Exit 69 for Duval Mine Road and you will be a few blocks from the Titan Missile Museum, a somber Cold War relic. The museum is an underground silo that contains a Titan missile minus its nuclear warhead. There were 54 intercontinental ballistic missile sites built around the United States between 1962 and 1984 — 18 of them around Tucson. The museum preserves the only one left in this area. Visitors can take one-hour guided tours. The museum, which is wheelchair accessible, is open every day, November through April, except Thanksgiving and

Towns & sites: Deadmen's Highway, Mission San Xavier del Bac, Titan Missile Museum, Green Valley, Madera Canyon, Santa Rita Mountains, Whipple Observatory, Tubac, Tumacacori National Monument, Nogales, Patagonia, and Sonoita.

Overview: Scenic panoramas and numerous points of interest and recreation sites line the route once called *El Camino de los Muertos* — Deadmen's Highway — between Tucson and Nogales.

Routes & mileage: Without side trips, about 145 miles via Interstate 19, State Route 82, State Route 83, and Interstate 10.

Time to allow: One or two days.

(OPPOSITE PAGE) *With the Mustang Mountains beyond, a stand of agaves spikes the rolling grasslands near Sonoita.* RANDY PRENTICE

(TOP) *Tumacacori National Historical Park offers special cultural programs during the cooler winter months. Here, men model typical garb of 18th-century Spanish presidio soldiers.* PATRICK FISCHER

(ABOVE) *The twin spires of Mission San Xavier del Bac catch the rosy glow of sunset.* LAURENCE PARENT

Christmas; from May to October, it's open Wednesday through Sunday.

Green Valley, the retirement town south of the museum, has numerous restaurants and places to shop. Green Valley is also the gateway to Madera Canyon in the Santa Rita Mountains, a popular outdoor recreation area in southern Arizona. To get there, take the Continental Exit (Exit 63), turn left (east) under the freeway, and continue 1.4 miles to East White House Canyon Road, which goes through a pecan grove. Follow that until you see Madera Canyon Road on your right. The paved road will cross three one-lane bridges, the third bridge spanning Florida Wash (pronounced floor-EE-dah). The bird-watchers among you will relish a walk up this wash.

Once over the wash, you will be facing the lush, pine-clad highlands of the Santa Ritas. Of the many trails in the area, one of my favorites begins in the Bog Springs campground, which you will see on your left. Park in the clearing next to the campground host. The Kent Springs Trail is a 5.4-mile route that climbs from the campground to Bog Springs, Kent Springs, and then heads down the mountain, passing Sylvester Spring before returning you to your starting point. You'll climb 1,800 feet in 2.7 miles

to Kent Springs and get wonderful views of Mount. Wrightson, at 9,453 feet the tallest peak in the range.

If you prefer not to hike, skip the campground and continue up Madera Canyon Road. Picnic at the various pull-outs up the canyon, or visit Santa Rita Lodge. Every weekday morning between March and September, the owners offer a four-hour bird walk starting at the lodge. Call in advance if you want to make the walk, because they never take more than eight people in a group, and there is a modest fee. The lodge also rents out rooms.

Among the many birds in Madera Canyon, you may see elegant trogons, rare parrot-like birds native to Mexico. The trogons arrive in the Santa Ritas around the first or second week of April and leave by September.

(ABOVE) *Clouds and sunlight cast dramatic colors across the Santa Rita Mountains and mesquite trees in a meadow near Madera Canyon south of Tucson.*
(OPPOSITE PAGE, ABOVE) *You can see Whipple Observatory's white domes from the highway.* BOTH BY RANDY PRENTICE
(OPPOSITE PAGE, BELOW) *Elephant Head protrudes from the Santa Rita foothills.* JACK DYKINGA

Backtrack down the canyon to I-19 and continue south about seven miles to Canoa Road (Exit 56). If astronomy interests you, you'll enjoy a visit to the Fred Lawrence Whipple Observatory, one of the largest field installations of the Smithsonian Institution Astrophysical Observatory.

The observatory is on 8,550-foot-high Mount Hopkins, but the visitors center is at the base of the mountain about 10 miles east of I-19. To get there, go left at the bottom of the Canoa Road exit ramp; turn right on the frontage road; continue south about three miles and turn left onto Elephant Head Road; and cross the bridge over the Santa Cruz River. A mile beyond the bridge, turn right onto Mount Hopkins Road. From there, it's seven miles to the visitors center. Food is not sold at the visitors center, but back on I-19, head south a short distance to Tubac, the next major site along the route, and you'll have a variety of restaurants from which to choose.

If you don't make any side trips, it is 45 miles from Tucson to Tubac, which bills itself as the town "Where Art and History Meet." Arizona's oldest European settlement, Tubac was once a Spanish *presidio*, or fort, that in recent years has grown into a colony where numerous artists and craftsman live and work.

Tubac is mainly a quaint tourist attraction, filled with art galleries and Southwestern-themed shops and appealingly small so that you can park anywhere and find everything you need within walking distance. Every February, dozens of arts and crafts vendors congregate for the Tubac Festival of the Arts, a colorful and entertaining weekend bazaar.

In the 1700s, Tubac was one of three Spanish presidios established in southern Arizona. Artifacts of the presidio and exhibits illustrating the history of the area can be found at Tubac Presidio State Historic Park and Museum east of the village's commercial center.

At the south side of the museum's parking lot, you can walk a 4.5-mile segment of the Anza National Historic Trail south along the Santa Cruz River to Tumacacori National Historical Park. The trail is named for Juan Bautista de Anza, the Tubac Presidio commander who in 1775 led a caravan of soldiers and families to

settle the San Francisco Bay area. Residents of the Tubac area re-enact the Anza expedition every October.

Leaving Tubac, you can return to I-19 and go down the freeway to Exit 29, or take the frontage road south four miles, to Tumacacori National Historical Park. A serene oasis with beautiful gardens and cultivated fields, the park preserves the ruins of a mission church that was used until 1848. Franciscan missionaries started building the church and associated structures in 1799. Funds ran short, and when the mission site was abandoned in 1848, the church building still hadn't been completed.

During the cooler months of the winter season, the park gives daily guided tours and can arrange for groups to take living history tours. This is the time of year when you can sometimes enjoy the mission by moonlight or watch arts and crafts demonstrations. The first weekend of every December, Tumacacori holds a two-day fiesta, and a special High Mass is conducted twice a year (costumes and reservations are required).

Across the road from Tumacacori's ruins, you'll find the Santa Cruz Chili and Spice Company and Ranch Museum, which is both a historic and aromatic delight.

In business since 1943, the company occupies an adobe building that was once part of an 19th-century land grant called the Baca Float Ranch. The museum displays antiques and bits of memorabilia from the ranch. If you enjoy Mexican flavors, the fragrance of natural spices, and chili products, the tiny store and museum is an experience you won't want to miss.

Back on the interstate, continue south about 13 miles to the State 289 interchange, which is Exit 12. If you'd like another excursion into the countryside, take State Route 289 west 9.3 miles to Peña Blanca Lake. The lake, a little over a mile long, offers a lush, quiet setting where you can go bird-watching, hike the easy two-mile trail around the shoreline, or shove off from the paved boat ramp and angle for fish.

Unfortunately, due to the lake's mercury contamination (probably the result of early-day prospecting operations), only the trout are edible; during the winter, they're stocked from hatcheries. Any other fish you may catch are too toxic to eat and must be released — you can't miss the posted warnings. Peña Blanca Lake currently has no amenities since the commercial services there — cabin rentals, lodge, restaurant, bar — went out of business. The nearby picnic grounds have tables and rest rooms, but no water; however, the campground down the road has rest rooms and running water.

When you return to the freeway, the twin cities of Nogales. Arizona, and Nogales, Mexico, are only seven miles further south.

Nogales is named for the walnut trees that once were an obvious part of the area's landscape. Now, what a visitor sees first are houses that appear perched precariously on the steep hills that flank the east and west sides of the busy downtown district. Throughout the year, Americans flood Obregon Avenue, the main street in the business district, in search of something distinctively Mexican. Obregon Avenue is literally lined for several blocks with gift shops that carry craft items from every state in Mexico, as well as domestic wines and liquors, porcelain from Germany, and perfumes from France.

Nothing in Tucson, or in the miles between Tucson and the border, prepares the visitor for the lively congestion and color or the commercial chaos that one finds in Nogales. There is, of course, a serious cultural life in Nogales, but most casual visitors are more likely to encounter a community that has become a commercial extravaganza — which is, in a way, why a day in Nogales is so entertaining.

Hawkers are usually placed in front of most stores and will lure you in with their promises of "Good prices on everything, amigo!" Prices are quoted in U.S. dollars, and the asking price in Nogales is rarely the final price. In fact, it is often twice the final price. The salesmen expect to haggle, and Americans have been known to express surprise at how rapidly and dramatically a price will drop. The

(OPPOSITE PAGE, TOP LEFT) *Walking in pioneer shoes for a day, these Tucson students tour Tubac Presidio State Park.* BOB & SUZANNE CLEMENZ

(OPPOSITE PAGE, TOP RIGHT) *Tubac, a green surprise in dry Arizona, enjoys a view of the Santa Ritas.* PATRICK FISCHER

(OPPOSITE PAGE, BOTTOM) *Tumacacori mission was founded by Father Eusebio Francisco Kino decades before the surviving church was built.* GEORGE H.H. HUEY

(ABOVE) *The shady cottonwoods and mesquites at Peña Blanca Lake invite picnicking.* RANDY PRENTICE

haggling is usually conducted in a light-hearted way. However, it is not considered good form to try to get a price reduced by criticizing workmanship or the quality of the materials used. Among the thousands of items you can find in Nogales are decorative sombreros, beautifully painted serving trays from Michoacan, masks from Guererro, baskets from Jalisco, silver candelabra from Puebla, woven wall hangings from Chiapas, embroidered dresses from Guadalajara, and ironwood carvings from Sonora.

When you've had your fill, you can retrace your route to Tucson or stay overnight in Nogales and return by a circuitous, scenic route through Patagonia. State Route 82 in Nogales, Arizona, also called the Patagonia Road, cuts a diagonal to the northeast, passing between the Patagonia and Santa Rita mountains. The route's second half provides some of the best views of the Santa Rita Mountains and the rolling grasslands of the Sonoita Valley. In Patagonia, the stunning Patagonia-Sonoita Creek Preserve, a great place to bird-watch or stroll, is just a couple of blocks west of the main road.

To return to Tucson, continue northeast on State Route 82 to the junction with State 83 in Sonoita, 11 miles beyond Patagonia. Turn left (north) on State Route 83, and 20 miles later, you'll be at Interstate 10. Turn west onto Interstate 10, and Tucson will appear in a few blinks. ◪

When You Go

Coronado National Forest: For information on Madera Canyon and the Santa Rita Mountains, call (520) 670-4552.

Nogales Chamber of Commerce: (520) 287-3685.

Patagonia Lake State Park: (520) 287-6965. Enter from State 82 between Patagonia and Nogales. Day-use and camping fees.

Patagonia-Sonoita Creek Preserve: (520) 394-2400. Limited roadside parking. Donations requested.

Pimería Alta Museum: Grand Avenue and Crawford Street in Nogales, Arizona. (520) 287-4621. No charge.

San Xavier del Bac: Open daily. No charge. (520) 294-2624.

Titan Missile Museum: (520) 625-7736. Tour reservations recommended. Admission fee.

Tubac Chamber of Commerce: (520) 398-2704.

Tubac Presidio State Historic Park: (520) 398-2252.

Metropolitan Tucson Convention & Visitors Center: (520) 624-1817 or (800) 638-8350.

Tumacacori National Historical Park: (520) 398-2341. Admission fee.

Whipple Observatory: (520) 670-5707. Reservations required for the six-hour bus tour from the visitors center. Tour fee.

Please see map on Page 119.

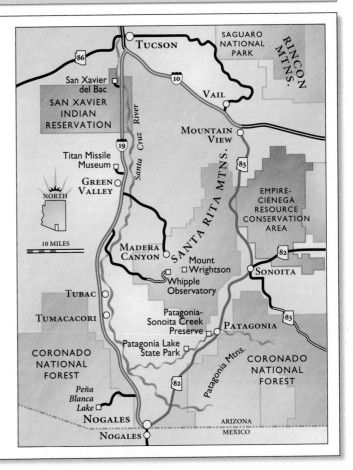

Getting Acquainted with the Old Pueblo

TUCSON REFLECTS THREE CULTURES

by Sam Negri

Tucson was first inhabited by Indians, later by Spaniards and Mexicans, and more recently by English-speaking settlers. A community of one sort or another has existed in what is now downtown Tucson since at least the seventh century.

In 1954, University of Arizona archaeologists found one wall of the Presidio of San Agustin del Tucson, established by the Royal Spanish Army in 1775. Down 18 inches from the base of the wall, they made a more dramatic discovery that opened a window to Tucson's distant past. The archaeologists had uncovered a hard-packed floor and the remains of an Indian pit house that had been part of a Hohokam Indian village. Radiocarbon dating of materials found at the site revealed that it had been occupied between A.D. 700 and 900.

Tucson is an anglicized version of *Chuk-son*, a Pima Indian word loosely translated as "foot of dark mountain." Chuk-son was an early Indian village at the base of Sentinel Peak, a cone-shaped hill near the Santa Cruz River. Sentinel usually is called "A" Mountain since each year students whitewash the huge letter on the hillside ("A" for the University of Arizona).

There is much to see and do around Tucson, and visitors can get a good feel for the area by driving up "A" Mountain and looking at the surrounding terrain. Drive to the west end of Congress Street and take the last left (south) turn just before Congress bends into Silverbell Road. The narrow paved road off Congress leads to a viewpoint near the top of "A" Mountain.

From the viewpoint, look to the right (south), and some 10 miles away, you'll see one of the most popular attractions in the area — Mission San Xavier del Bac. Many believe the city's link to its historic past is best felt at this restored and active mission on the San Xavier Indian Reservation. Known as "The White Dove of the Desert," the mission was established by the Jesuit priest Eusebio Francisco Kino in 1700. The original church and a second church were destroyed. The mission church that exists today is believed to have been completed in 1797.

Still used by the Tohono O'odham Indians, San Xavier del Bac is a beautifully restored architectural gem, often valued as much for its stunning art work as for its religious life. Admission is free to this place of beauty and worship, but donations are appreciated. Throughout the day, a tape-recorded narrative recounts the history of the mission and its place in the lives of the native inhabitants. There's also a gift shop attached to the east side of

Overview: When people around Arizona talk about Tucson, sooner or later they mention that the state's second largest city has a unique feel about it. What they mean, usually, is that while many cities have seemingly obscured their roots in the push toward metropolis, the charm of cultural heritage of the Old Pueblo — as it's often called — remains almost palpable. As the city continues to grow, that claim seems to be more a state of mind than a condition of reality, and yet, with relatively little effort, it still is possible to find physical links to the three cultures that have shaped the city's history.

(OPPOSITE PAGE) *The moon floats over busy Congress Street, the downtown Tucson skyline, and the darkened Rincon Mountains beyond.* RANDY PRENTICE
(TOP) *El Tiradito is a legendary wishing shrine in downtown Tucson.* EDWARD McCAIN
(ABOVE) *Much loving labor has reclaimed the beauty of the luminous artwork at the Mission San Xavier del Bac, which still serves the Tohono O'odham.* RICHARD MAACK

the church where you can find religious and historical items as well as beautiful baskets woven by Tohono O'odham women.

Back at our perch on "A" Mountain, look directly east across the Santa Cruz River to the tall buildings in downtown Tucson. Some of the buildings occupy the site of the frontier presidio established on August 20, 1775.

El Presidio Park, in front of City Hall, constituted the southern half of the presidio and was the Plaza de Las Armas. Directly to the left (north) of City Hall and the Tucson Museum of Art lies El Presidio Historic District, a neighborhood of once-elegant homes built by pioneer businessmen between the latter part of the 19th century and the early decades of the 20th century. A walking tour map of the district is available from the Tucson Convention & Visitors Bureau.

Walking the quiet streets of El Presidio provides a good feel for what Tucson was like at the turn of the century. Two of the more notable restorations in the neighborhood in recent years are the graceful facade of the Owls Club, an ornate turn-of-the-century boarding home for bachelors (now occupied by a civil engineering company), and the ornate Steinfeld Mansion, once owned by a pioneer business leader and now occupied by law offices. Some of the lesser institutions of the district, including a bordello called "Cribs of the Sisters of the Ancient Sorority," have vanished.

From "A" Mountain, it's easy to see that Tucson lies on a large, relatively flat plain surrounded by five mountain ranges — the Catalinas and Tortolitas on the north, the Rincons on the east, the Tucson Mountains on the west, and the Santa Ritas some 40 miles to the south. The base of these ranges provides much of what most visitors find captivating about Tucson.

For example, drive down "A" Mountain and head north for a few blocks on Silverbell Road to Anklam Road and turn left (west) into the Tucson Mountains. Five miles later, you'll find yourself at the narrow cut called Gates Pass, a spot where you will have a breathtaking view of the

dense saguaro forest protected in Tucson Mountain Park (a county park) and Saguaro National Park (West).

Before Saguaro National Park, though, you'll reach two other major Tucson attractions first. The famous movie location, Old Tucson Studios, and the Arizona-Sonora Desert Museum are located on Kinney Road in Tucson Mountain Park.

Old Tucson Studios is a theme park and movie set. Columbia Pictures built the set in 1939 for the movie *Arizona*, with William Holden, Jean Arthur, Rita Hayworth, and Glenn Ford. Many familiar movies and television series have since been filmed there, including *Winchester 73* (1950), with Jimmy Stewart, and *Tombstone* (1993), with Val Kilmer and Kurt Russell. In 1995, a night-time fire that was visible across much of the city destroyed 40 percent of the buildings at Old Tucson, taking with it an enormous treasure of Western memorabilia. After reconstruction, the park reopened in 1997. Live shows are performed all day — shoot-outs, magic shows, dance hall revues. There are rides and games for kids, restaurants, and souvenir shops; and everything looks just a bit as Tucson probably looked in the 1880s.

The Arizona-Sonora Desert Museum is few miles north of Old Tucson. Except for its large parking lot, the museum blends into its natural surroundings. The desert museum is not a museum in the conventional sense. Nearly everything there is an outdoor exhibit, and it is as much a zoo and botanical garden as it is a museum, surrounding the visitor with the Sonoran Desert's plants and animals — at a safe distance, of course. Its design set a standard for similar institutions the world over.

Walking its graceful paths, you'll easily get the impression you are visiting the birds, bighorn sheep, packrats, coyotes, and bears in their natural habitat. Allow at least a few hours to visit the desert museum. Strollers and wheelchairs are available.

The Saguaro National Park's Red Hills Information Center is about a mile north of the desert museum. This is the park's west unit; the other unit is on Tucson's far east side, each section with its own visitors center.

In the west unit, there are easy trails and a loop drive that begins at the visitors center. One trail, on the Bajada Loop Drive three miles north of the visitors center, meanders through a cactus forest so dense that experts estimate an average of 15,000 to 20,000 saguaros grow per square mile. If you're traveling with children, you can get activity

packs for them to take on a walk through the adjacent wash. Together you can look for the animal tracks, birds, and plants listed.

For a fascinating reminder of Tucson's antiquity, take a drive to the park's Signal Hill picnic ground and follow the path to the rocky hill at the northeast end of the parking area. The rough volcanic rocks that cover the hill are etched with petroglyphs, ancient Indian drawings of desert animals and various symbols depicting rain and lightning.

On another day — you can't see everything Tucson has to offer in one day — head to the other end of town. Drive east to Tanque Verde Road, turn left (north), and go to Sabino Canyon Road. Turn left on Sabino Canyon Road, and you'll end up in the Sabino Canyon Recreation Area, a part of the Coronado National Forest.

Sabino Canyon is a stunning contrast to the saguaro-studded hills around it. Watered most of the year by a creek starting high in the Santa Catalina Mountains, the canyon is a scenic oasis of sycamore, ash, and pine trees growing at the base of cliffs more than 2,000 feet high. Open-air trams leave the visitors center for narrated tours, meandering 3.8 miles up the canyon on a paved road that crosses nine stone bridges. No other vehicles are allowed in the canyon.

For many Tucsonans, the mountain range rising above Sabino Canyon — the 200-square-mile Santa Catalina Mountains — provides a refreshing oasis of campgrounds and picnic areas, an alpine village, and even a ski area just one hour from the center of the city. Locals may casually refer to the Catalinas in general as Mount Lemmon, after its tallest peak (9,157 feet), named

for botanist John Gill Lemmon, who came here in 1881.

Taking the serpentine paved road up the mountain, you'll have to pay a per-vehicle toll in the vicinity of Molino Basin. The road is open all year — there's the village of Summerhaven at 7,500 feet, and Ski Valley is 500 feet above that — but in the winter months, chains may be required if there's been a lot of snow.

At Summerhaven, you'll find restaurants, cabins for rent, and souvenir shops. You can also drive through the village to Marshall Gulch, where there's a picnic area set among the ponderosa pines, as well as excellent trails that lead deeper into an aspen forest. The chair lifts that carry skiers to the top of Ski Valley in the winter months provide scenic rides during the summer.

For this Mount Lemmon excursion, drive east on Grant Road to Tanque Verde Road, then go left on Tanque Verde to the Catalina Highway. Go left again on the Catalina Highway. In about 25 miles, you'll be deep in a forest of pine, aspen, and fir trees. Roll down the car windows and breathe in the cool, fresh air. Further along, at Windy Point, you'll get a panoramic view for some 50 miles, and at Rose Canyon's small lake, you can fish for trout.

If the trip up the mountain makes anything clear, it is that Tucson is a place of startling contrasts, where glass and concrete skyscrapers tower a few miles away from pre-Columbian archaeological sites and skiers can frolic in the snow less than an hour away from desert habitats. The contrast becomes sharply surreal about 45 miles north of

(LEFT) *The winding Catalina, or Mount Lemmon, Highway loops near Geology Vista.* PETER NOEBELS
(BELOW) *Outside Oracle, Columbia University's Biosphere II Center looks like a vision of the future.* EDWARD McCAIN

Tucson, where a startlingly futuristic complex dominates the Santa Catalina foothills.

Biosphere II, located just outside the town of Oracle, is basically a three-acre greenhouse duplicating the earth's major ecosystems. Like an enormous terrarium sectioned into a rain forest, an ocean with a beach, a fog desert, a tropical savanna, and an agricultural bay, it's a world within a world, all under glass and meant to be self-sustaining. In 1991, eight scientists were sealed inside for a two-year research project, which ended somewhat controversially. Now a campus for Columbia University's Earth Institute, the Biosphere II Center's faculty and students are studying the effects of increased carbon dioxide in a carefully regulated environment, but you can watch the undersea life in the enclosed ocean and visit the human habitat where the original "biospherians" were isolated. The complex includes a hotel, conference center, gift shops, and restaurant. ▼

When You Go

Arizona Historical Society Museum: 949 E. Second St., (520) 628-5774. Donations welcome.

Arizona-Sonora Desert Museum: (520) 883-1380. Admission fee.

Arizona State Museum: Park Avenue and University Blvd., University of Arizona. (520) 621-6281. No charge.

Biosphere II: Oracle. (520) 896-6200 or (800) 828-2462. Admission fee. Web site: *www.bio2.edu/*

Tucson Children's Museum: 200 S. Sixth Ave. in the historic Carnegie building. (520) 792-9985. Admission fee.

Flandrau Science Center/Planetarium: University of Arizona. (520) 621-7827 or 621-4515. Admission and show fees.

Mission San Xavier del Bac: (520) 294-2624. No charge.

Old Tucson Studios: (520) 883-0100. Admission fee.

Pima Air and Space Museum: 6000 E. Valencia Road, near Tucson International Airport. (520) 574-0462. Admission fee.

Sabino Canyon: Coronado National Forest, (520) 749-8700. No charge for admission, but you pay a fare for the optional tram rides.

Saguaro National Park: (520) 733-5100. West unit, (520) 733-5158. West unit has no entry fee, but east unit does.

Metropolitan Tucson Convention & Visitors Bureau: (520) 624-1817 or (800) 638-8350.

Tucson Museum of Art and Historic Block: 140 N. Main Ave., (520) 624-2333. Admission fee.

University of Arizona Museum of Art: (520) 621-7567. No admission charge, but most parking is metered or in pay lots.

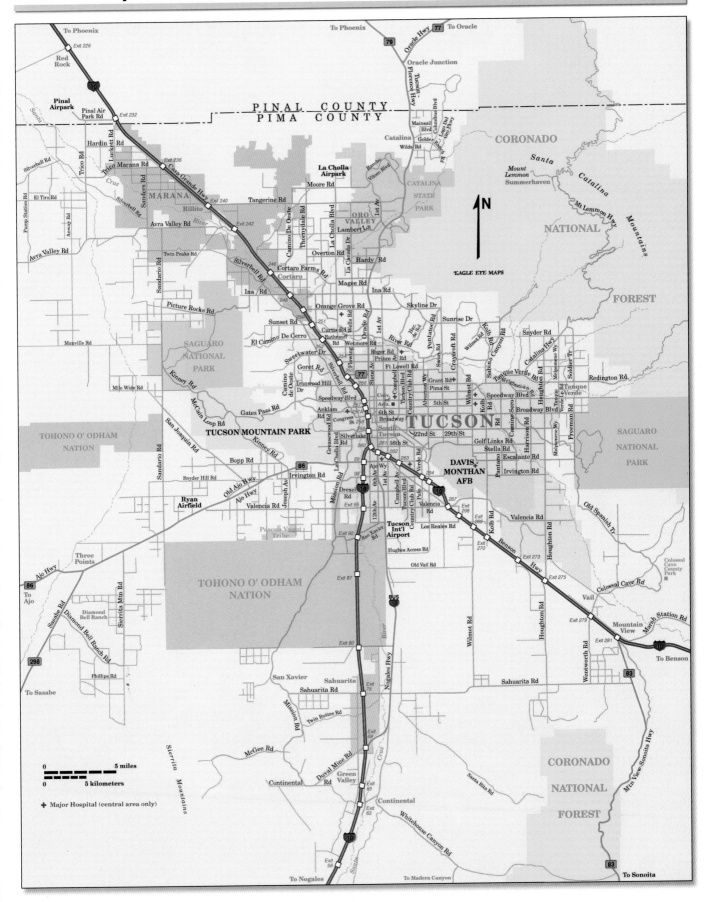

Outdoors in Tucson

HIKES, BIKES, AND THE LIKE

by Sam Negri

With an approximate population of 800,000, Tucson ranks second among Arizona cities. It lies in a natural bowl 2,390 feet above sea level and is surrounded by five mountain ranges — the Santa Catalina and Tortolita mountains on the north, the Rincons on the east, the Tucson Mountains on the west, and the Santa Rita Mountains about 40 miles to the south.

The sun shines approximately 300 days in any given year, and from November to late April, Tucson's climate is close to perfect. While temperatures on winter mornings and nights can drop to 40° F. and sometimes lower, the mercury will likely rise to between 50° and 70° (and sometimes higher) during the day.

Very popular among golfing enthusiasts because of its climate, Tucson has a number of desert-landscaped courses designed by such big-name golfers as Robert Trent Jones Jr., Tom Weiskopf, Arthur Hills, and Jack Nicklaus.

Summer temperatures are another story. During July, the hottest month of year, temperatures will average 100° during the day and seldom drop below 80° at night. August, one of the wettest months, isn't much cooler. In the summer months, many residents head for the forests and campgrounds in the Santa Catalina Mountains, the long barrier across metropolitan Tucson's northern edge. Hard-core golf fanatics still hit the greens, but often in the earlier morning hours.

Combine what the mountains have to offer with an abundance of city parks, and you can find everything from a flat, easy place to stroll to steep and extremely demanding mountain trails. In some areas — Sabino Canyon and Saguaro National Park, in particular — you can avoid hiking altogether and spend a leisurely morning sight-seeing from a tram (Sabino) or your car (both east and west units of Saguaro). Saguaro National Park is divided into two large sections, the Tucson Mountain District on the city's far west side and the Rincon Mountain District on the far east side. Each unit has its own visitors center offering key information about the park trails and drives.

Overview: Five mountain ranges, saguaro forests, parks, and canyons bring the outdoors right into Tucson. Tucson's setting — a broad valley where tall saguaro cactuses seem to be marching to and from one mountain range or another — coupled with an omnipresent blue sky and excellent visibility, can make a person feel guilty about staying indoors too long. The larger mountain ranges around the city are protected as national forests or national parks, and there are endless opportunities to get out and hike, backpack, go bird-watching, mountain-biking, rock climbing, skiing, or golfing.

(LEFT) *On the northeastern edge of Tucson, Sabino Creek has recreational opportunities for everyone — even bookworms.* DAVID LAZAROFF
(ABOVE, RIGHT) *Only the hardy and fit make it to this exclusive cookout on Hitchcock Pinnacle.* PETER NOEBELS
(RIGHT) *Desert golf has prickly hazards.* EDWARD McCAIN

In Saguaro's west unit in the Tucson Mountains, the Red Hills Information Center can be used as a jumping-off point for two easy nature trails.

If you're traveling with kids, ask for an activity pack at the visitors center. Your child will receive a bright knapsack containing binoculars, a ruler, colored pencils, and a coloring book with pictures and questions about the plants and animals that can be seen in the desert. Following the instructions in the book and the accompanying literature, children can wander in the desert, listing animals and plants they've seen and identifying animal tracks and birds. The activity book has plenty to color, some connect-the-dots-pictures, a crossword puzzle, and more, which children can complete while they walk the short nature trails around the visitors center. It's an entertaining way for children and their parents to learn more about the Sonoran Desert.

While there are numerous trails in the Tucson Mountains, one of the most popular and accessible is the 2.3-mile King Canyon Trail, which begins across the road from the entrance to the Arizona-Sonora Desert Museum and leads to Sweetwater Saddle. From the saddle, where you'll have a fantastic view to the west of Avra Valley and the Tohono O'odham Reservation in the distance, you can keep climbing to 4,687-foot Wasson Peak or meander back down to the trailhead.

Not too steep (it involves an elevation gain of only 1,000 feet), King Canyon Trail offers superior opportunities for wildlife viewing. It's one of those rare spots in the desert where there is a semi-reliable spring. Such spots predictably attract the thirsty — in this case, coyotes, mountain lions, mule deer, skunks, javelina, ground squirrels, and a wide variety of birds.

Saguaro National Park's east unit — the Rincon Mountain District — is another embarrassment of riches as far as trails are concerned. For some easy hikes in the desert, drive to the east end of Broadway Boulevard. The Cactus Forest Trail begins on Broadway a quarter mile east of Freeman Road at an elevation of about 2,700 feet. The trailhead looks like a V. The path to your left is marked Shantz Trail and leads to a spot called Pink Hill. The trail, which is practically flat, winds between typical plants of the Sonoran Desert: giant saguaro, cholla, and barrel cactuses and palo-verde and mesquite trees. Walk 0.3 of a mile on the Shantz until you see a marker for the Pink Hill Trail. Turn east (or right) another 0.8 of a mile, still barely gaining any elevation, and you'll come to the junction of the Loma Verde Trail. At that point you can either continue east for a half-mile over the top of Pink Hill, or you can go left a half mile and make a loop that connects the Pink Hill Trail with the Loma Verde and Wentworth trails. The Wentworth leads back to the Shantz. This shortens the hike from a 4.5-mile loop to a three-mile loop.

Saguaro's east unit also is the gateway to a wonderful wilderness area in the roadless high country of the Rincon Mountains. The trail that begins at the east end of Speedway Boulevard climbs from the desert to Douglas Spring (which is dry) and a grove of juniper and oak trees. While extraordinarily beautiful and very popular, this trail is not for everyone. It's 5.9 miles to Douglas Spring over some steep grades forming an elevation gain of 2,100 feet. If you're on a backpacking trip, you can camp at Douglas Spring (permit required) or continue the steep climb to Cowhead Saddle and Manning Camp, seven miles beyond Douglas Spring. By the time you get to Manning Camp (where drinking water is available), you'll be in ponderosa pines.

Aside from Manning Camp and a couple of other places where there are springs, the area is bone dry. In the winter months, carry one or two quarts of water per person for each day you'll be out.

Sabino Canyon, at the base of the Santa Catalina Mountains, dramatically contrasts with what you'll see at Saguaro National Park. The cliffs that separate Sabino from neighboring Bear Canyon rise 2,500 feet from a stream that carries water most of the year (many Arizona streams are often dry). The stream, lined with sycamore, cottonwood, and ash trees, is crisscrossed by nine low stone bridges and a paved road that meanders 3.8 miles up the canyon. However, the only motorized traffic allowed on this road is provided by a tram that takes visitors on a 45-minute excursion up the canyon from the small visitors center. Several steep trails begin in lower Sabino, or you can ride to the end of the route and take

(OPPOSITE PAGE, ABOVE) *In the foreground of this wash at Saguaro National Park (West), a mule deer buck is barely visible among the giant saguaros.* TOM DANIELSEN
(OPPOSITE PAGE, BELOW) *The Tucson Mountains offer trails to suit almost everyone's stamina.* EDWARD McCAIN
(ABOVE, RIGHT) *King Canyon's stream creates good wildlife-spotting opportunities.* PETER NOEBELS
(RIGHT) *Sabino Canyon's creekside serenity is minutes from metropolitan Tucson.* DAVID LAZAROFF

the trail up to Hutch's Pool (a natural catchment in the rocks above Sabino) and beyond.

To get to Sabino Canyon, drive east to Tanque Verde Road, turn left and take Tanque Verde to Sabino Canyon Road, then turn left there and 4.5 miles on Sabino Canyon Road to Sabino Canyon Recreation Area. From the parking lot, you can either walk or pay to ride the tram into the canyon.

You also pay for a separate shuttle that leaves the same area and goes 2.5 miles into lower Bear Canyon and the trailhead for Seven Falls. The relatively flat, 2.2-mile (one-way) hike to Seven Falls is very popular. In the spring, when Sabino Creek swells with melted snow, you can watch the creek cascade over a tall, terraced cliff at Seven Falls. Bear Canyon is also home to one of the largest-known Arizona cypresses — 93 feet tall and

measuring 20 feet in circumference at shoulder height. Along the trail, you'll pass scattered ponderosa and Chihuahua pines.

In the Santa Catalinas above Sabino Canyon, the tallest peak is Mount Lemmon, reaching 9,157 feet. The Catalina, or Mount Lemmon, Highway is a paved toll road running all the way up the south face of the Catalinas Mount Lemmon's summit. The Catalinas offer an escape from the intense summer heat, and Tucson residents use the campgrounds and picnic areas on the mountain extensively from Memorial Day through Labor Day.

The highway twists and loops its way up the mountain, first to the village of Summerhaven and then the ski slopes beyond at 8,000 feet. Summerhaven is small, but you can rent a cabin, shop for such domestic necessities as pot holders and ceramic mugs, and indulge yourself with homemade pie and "Mount Lemmonade."

For a few months during the winter, you can ski at Mount Lemmon Ski Valley, the southernmost ski slopes in the United States. During the summer, you can ride the lifts for a breathtaking view of the pine and aspen forests at the top of the range.

If you're looking for a good half-day hike, drive through Summerhaven to Marshall Gulch, where the road ends. The Aspen Trail begins next to the rest rooms. You can make a two-mile loop on the Aspen Trail or continue deeper into the mountain in Lemmon Spring and the Wilderness of Rocks.

To get to the Catalina Highway, take Grant Road east to Tanque Verde Road, go left on Tanque Verde to the Catalina Highway. Go left again on the Catalina Highway. After about 25 miles, the forest encompasses you. Be ready to pay the toll at Milepost 5, just below Molino Basin.

(LEFT) *The chunky buttresses of Bear Canyon Arch near Tucson glow red at sunset.*
(RIGHT) *At Seven Falls, Sabino Creek spills into a series of waterfalls over steep terraces.*
BOTH BY JACK DYKINGA

As the highway climbs from the desert, the saguaros and manzanita bushes give way to oaks and junipers at 4,500 feet. At 6,623 feet, stop the car for a little gawking at Windy Point. Maybe experiment with that panoramic setting on your camera, because the eagle-eye view extends for about 50 miles. One of the rest area's granite boulders has a map that will orient you to the many mountains unfolding at the edges of the desert floor. You'll also more than likely encounter rock climbers with their cleats and ropes, ready to practice scaling some of the sheer rock walls at Windy Point.

The Santa Rita Mountains, like the Santa Catalinas, rise from the desert floor to slightly higher than 9,000 feet. The Santa Ritas are an easy 40-mile drive south of Tucson's city limits.

Madera Canyon, the main access point in the range, is accessible by a paved road. The range is laced with wonderful trails — the Super Trail at the top of Madera Canyon will lead you to 9,453-foot-high Mount Wrightson on a relatively gentle route through cool pine forests. Madera Canyon is the best-known birding spot in Arizona, possibly because, as *A Birders Guide to Southeastern Arizona* reports: "Madera Canyon is the

(OPPOSITE PAGE, ABOVE) *The sun pins a faint rainbow against a storm rising beyond Windy Point on the Catalina Highway.* PETER NOEBELS
(OPPOSITE PAGE, BELOW) *This road leads to Helvetia, a copper mining ghost town in the Santa Ritas.*
GEORGE STOCKING
(RIGHT) *Sycamore leaves sprinkle a stream in the Santa Ritas' Madera Canyon.* DAVID MUENCH

nearest (to Tucson) and easiest place to see the full panoply of Sierra Madrean hummingbirds, elegant trogon, sulphur-bellied flycatcher, and other pine/oak woodland specialties confined to the border ranges. If you have time to bird only a single location in spring or summer, visit Madera Canyon."

Madera Canyon has many side roads that are good for mountain biking. For instance, as you drive into the canyon, watch for a sign on the right for Elephant Head Road. An old mining road that leads through Chino Valley, it passes the base of a gigantic rock that resembles an elephant's head.

To get to Madera Canyon from Tucson, take I-10 to I-19 and turn south on I-19. Just 23.5 miles south on the interstate, take Exit 63 at Continental. Turn left (east) under the freeway and continue to East White House Canyon Road (1.4 miles), located halfway through a bend in the middle of a pecan grove, until you see Madera Canyon Road on your right. This paved road soon passes over three narrow bridges. ◪

When You Go

Catalina State Park: (520) 628-5798. Admission fee.

Colossal Cave Mountain Park: (520) 647-7275. South of Saguaro National Park (East). Admission fee. Trail rides, guided tours extra.

Madera Canyon: Coronado National Forest, Nogales District, (520) 281-2296.

Mount Lemmon: Use fees vary. Coronado National Forest, Santa Catalina District, (520) 749-8700.

Mount Lemmon Ski Valley: (520) 576-1400.

Sabino Canyon: Coronado National Forest, (520) 749-8700. No charge except fares for optional narrated tram rides.

Saguaro National Park: (520) 733-5100. East unit has entry fee, (520) 733-5153; west unit (no entry fee), (520) 733-5158.

Metropolitan Tucson Convention & Visitors Bureau: (800) 638-8350 or (520) 624-1817.

Tucson Mountain Park: Pima County Parks, (520) 740-2680.

Please see map on Page 119.

Getting Acquainted with Central Phoenix

by Joe Stocker

Overview: This, the first of four chapters dealing primarily with attractions in an area commonly called the Valley of the Sun (or "the Valley"), focuses on sites in downtown Phoenix, the city's central corridor, south and west sides, the Glendale area, and the northern fringes. Although the sites are listed in accordance with their locations, the presentation is not a tour. Before setting out to visit the sites, readers are urged to call the telephone numbers at the end of each listing to check on visiting hours and admission fees, if any. The other three chapters deal with east Phoenix, Tempe, Mesa, Scottsdale, and other east Valley areas; recreation areas for hiking, bicycling, and other outdoor pursuits; and Indian history and culture.

Phoenix ranks as the seventh-largest U.S. city, with more than 1.2 million living in an area bigger than Los Angeles. Count the satellite cities and towns, one flowing into the next throughout the Salt River Valley, and the metropolitan population exceeds 2.9 million.

The Valley's first inhabitants were prehistoric Indians lured by the Salt River's abundant water. They settled here perhaps as early as 200 B.C. and dug an extensive network of irrigation canals. Later, the Valley's Akimel O'odham, or Pima Indians, named those first settlers the Hohokam (generally said "ho-ho-KAM"), meaning "all used up," "departed," or "gone away." The Hohokam simply disappeared around the 15th and early 16th centuries.

In the mid-1800s, European settlers joined the Pimas. They re-dug the Hohokam's canals and grew hay for the U.S. Army. One of those pioneers, a bibulous, poetic Englishman named Darrell Duppa, talked about the legendary phoenix bird rising from its own ashes. Here in the ruins of a lost Indian civilization, he said, it would happen again. It did, and Duppa is remembered as the man who gave Phoenix its name.

Four developments transformed that modest farming community into the dynamic metropolis that it is today.

• In 1911, the federal government built Theodore Roosevelt Dam on the Salt River. More dams followed on the Salt and the converging Verde River, and the Valley became an agricultural center. In recent years, water from the Colorado River has helped quench the Valley's thirst.

• With the automobile's arrival, the warm desert winters drew tourists, who spurred the growth of resorts.

• World War II brought military bases, defense plants, and people to staff them. After the war, many of those troops and workers settled in the Valley.

• Refrigerated air conditioning supplanted evaporative coolers — swamp coolers, folks called them. With that, summers became bearable.

Now, let's look at places that you should consider visiting. Addresses and phone numbers follow each listing.

(LEFT) *Despite high-rise buildings, mountains are visible from the central corridor.* DAVID H. SMITH
(ABOVE) *Trees, parks, and open space soften Phoenix's downtown setting.* RICHARD MAACK
(RIGHT) *The restored Orpheum Theater retains trappings of the early 20th century.* DAVID H. SMITH

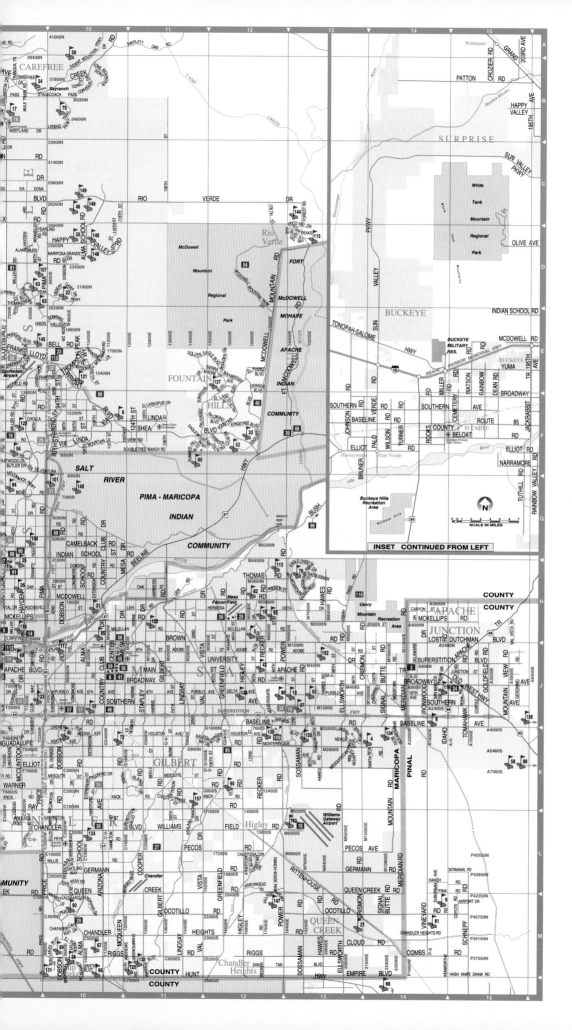

INSET CONTINUED FROM LEFT

LEGEND

- 🚩 **GOLF COURSES**
- 10 **POINTS OF INTEREST**
- 1 **MAJOR SHOPPING**
- ✚ **HOSPITALS**
- C **COUNTY BLDGS.**
- F **FEDERAL BLDGS.**
- M **MUNICIPAL BLDGS.**
- L **LIBRARIES**
- P **POST OFFICES**

Phoenix and the West Side

For east-west streets, address numbering originates at Central Avenue. For example, 120 W. Thomas Road is one block west of Central. For north-south streets, numbering begins at Washington Street. For example, 3063 N. 16th St. is 30 blocks north of Washington.

Red numbers followed by N, S, E, or W indicate the number of blocks a street is from Central or Washington.

Even-numbered addresses are on the north or west side of streets. Odd numbers are on the south or east. Numbered "avenues" and "drives" run parallel to and west of Central. Numbered "streets" and "places" are east of Central.

Several major streets change name as they move away from the central core. Glendale Avenue becomes Lincoln Drive as it heads east from the Squaw Peak Parkway; to avoid mountains, Thunderbird Road dips south for awhile and follows the course of Cactus Road. Dunlap Avenue in Phoenix turns into Olive Avenue after crossing 39th Avenue

The East Valley

North-south streets in Paradise Valley, Scottsdale, Chandler, and Gilbert continue the numbering pattern established in Phoenix.

In Tempe, most numbered streets run east-west and parallel to the Salt River, with First Street immediately south of the river. Mill Avenue begins numbering for east-west streets.

In Mesa, Center and Main streets are the zero points for street numbering. Lower numbered streets run east-west in the downtown area. Higher numbered streets are found east of downtown and run north-south.

Several major streets undergo name changes as they go from one city to another. Apache Boulevard in Tempe becomes Main Street in Mesa and eventually turns into the Apache Trail as it heads east. University Drive starts in Tempe, goes through Mesa, and turns into Superstition Boulevard after being bisected by the Apache Trail in Apache Junction. Scottsdale Road becomes Rural Road when it enters Tempe. Hayder Road in Scottsdale becomes McClintock Road in Tempe after crossing the Salt River. Country Club Drive in Mesa becomes Arizona Avenue in Chandler.

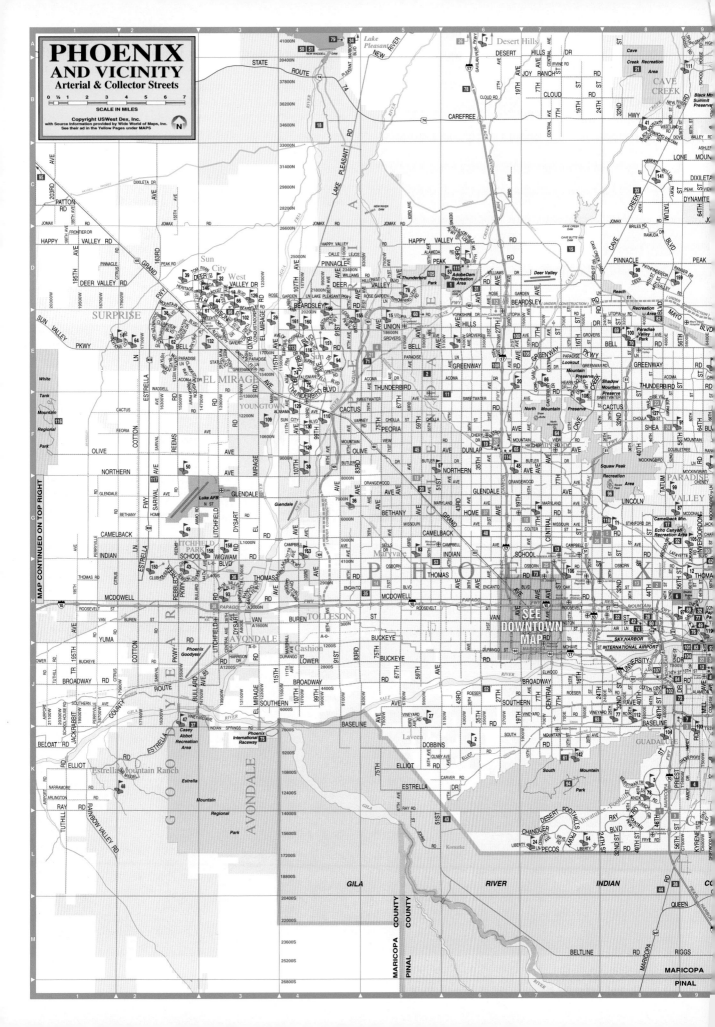

Many listings include a site number and grid coordinates corresponding to the foldout map following Page 130 (map courtesy of Qwest Dex).

PATRIOTS SQUARE PARK: A 2.5-acre, globe-lighted greensward, dominated by a 115-foot spire. Brown-baggers gather here for lunch, and often you can catch a mid-day concert of one kind or another on an outdoor stage sheltered by a ship's-sail roof. The park hosts events like St. Patrick's Day and Cinco de Mayo celebrations and rallies before downtown sports events. The park caps an underground garage. Washington Street and Central Avenue. (602) 262-6412. (#17, C-3, downtown inset)

ORPHEUM THEATER: A deliciously glitzy (twinkling stars and moving clouds in the ceiling) theater built in 1929. Languished until the Junior League and the city restored it. Now a gorgeous Spanish baroque venue for national touring companies. Reserve a free tour. 203 E. Adams St. (602) 252-9678. (#16, C-3, downtown)

MUSEO CHICANO: Imaginative gallery focusing on Mexican-American and Mexican art, but including other Latin American cultures. Events explore literature, music, and food. Admission fee. 147 E. Adams St. (602) 257-5536. (#15, C-3, downtown)

AMERICA WEST ARENA: Home for the Phoenix Suns (basketball), Phoenix Coyotes (hockey), Arizona Rattlers (arena football), and Phoenix Mercury (women's basketball). Concerts and circuses also. Food court handy for lunch. 201 E. Jefferson St. (602) 379-7800. (#1, C-3, downtown)

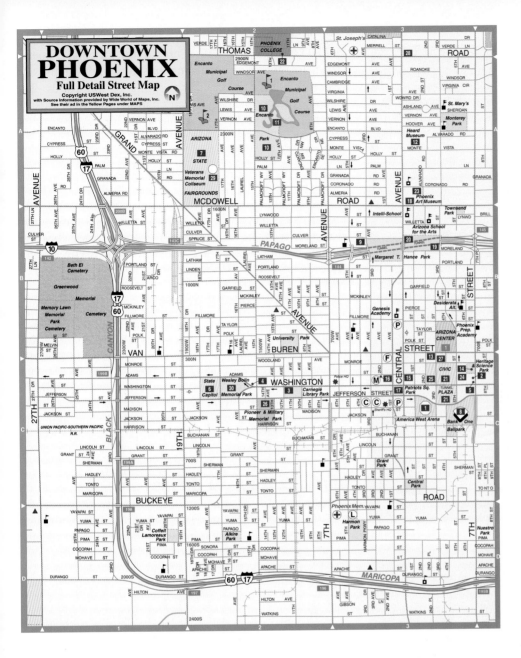

DOWNTOWN PHOENIX
Full Detail Street Map

Copyright USWest Dex, Inc.
with Source Information provided by Wide World of Maps, Inc.
See their ad in the Yellow Pages under MAPS

(OPPOSITE PAGE, TOP LEFT) *America West Arena is more than the venue for professional basketball, arena football, concerts, and special events. Its food court is a handy lunch spot for downtown workers and visitors.* DAVID H. SMITH (OPPOSITE PAGE, TOP RIGHT AND BOTTOM) *Bank One Ballpark, whimsically called BOB, sports a retractable dome that keeps fans watching baseball in air-conditioned comfort and allows the desert sunshine to nourish the field's natural grass.* KERRICK JAMES AND DAVID H. SMITH

BANK ONE BALLPARK: The nearly 50,000-seat, air-conditioned home of Major League Baseball's Arizona Diamondbacks features a retractable roof, restaurants and food concessions, a picnic ground — even a swimming pool. 401 E. Jefferson St. (602) 514-8400. (#8, C-3, downtown)

PHOENIX POLICE MUSEUM: The kids can climb into a patrol car, flick on the lights, and listen to the radio. Other features include a Model T Ford, a video on gun safety, and replicas of jail cells. 101 S. Central Ave., Suite 100. (602) 534-7278. (C-3, downtown)

PHOENIX CIVIC PLAZA: The Civic Plaza area is downtown's convention and entertainment center, with five exhibit halls, a ballroom, a multi-purpose stage, and 43 meeting rooms. Architectural styles and decor reflect prehistoric Indian cultures. The plaza is as long as 6.5 football fields — long enough for a small plane to take off. Symphony Hall houses the Phoenix

Symphony, a major orchestra with full-time players; the Arizona Opera; and national touring shows. The Herberger Theater Center across the street has two auditoriums, enabling it to accommodate several theater companies. The larger auditorium's orchestra pit can be lowered hydraulically for additional seating or extended sets. Out front, you'll see John Waddell's sculpted lithe, bronze ballet dancers. Symphony Hall, 225 E. Adams St. (602) 262-6225. (#21, C-3, downtown) Herberger Theater, 222 E. Monroe St. (602) 254-7399. (#13, C-3, downtown)

ARIZONA CENTER: A melange of office towers, restaurants, shops, bars, marketplace carts, and a multiplex movie theater artfully blend with fountains and garden space; designed and built by the Maryland company that renovated Baltimore's waterfront and the area around Faneuil Hall in Boston. Van Buren and Third streets. (602) 271-4000 or 949-4386. (B-3, downtown)

ST. MARY'S BASILICA: Established in 1881, the basilica is Phoenix's oldest church building still in use. Monroe and Third streets. (602) 252-7651. (#27, C-3, downtown)

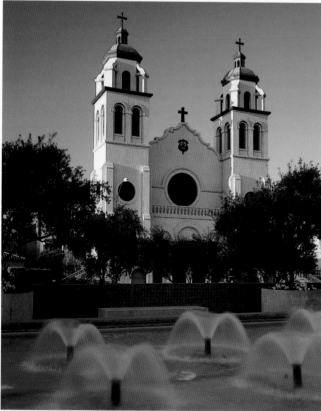

HERITAGE SQUARE: Part of the original Phoenix townsite, this block features museums, gift shops, and eateries housed in buildings dating to the 1880s. The main attraction is a Victorian charmer, the 1895 Rosson House, built by an early-day physician for $7,500; admission fee. In the venerable Stevens house, you'll find the Arizona Doll and Toy Museum, featuring miniature dollhouses, a schoolroom display, and dolls depicting Canada's Dionne quintuplets; admission fee. Built in 1900, the three-bedroom Silva House, maintained by the Salt River Project, was one of Phoenix's first homes wired for electricity; no charge. Hours vary for each location; some summer closures. Monroe and Sixth streets. Recording, (602) 262-5029; city office, (602) 262-5071. (#14, C-3, downtown)

ARIZONA SCIENCE CENTER: The facility features a potpourri of exhibits and demonstrations, including a planetarium and giant-screen iWerks theater. You can explore the universe, follow astronauts through their training, "fly" an airplane, learn how to beat the Arizona heat, get acquainted with ham radio networks, and fiddle with many other interactive demonstrations and exhibits dealing with physics, life sciences, health, and minerals. Admission fee; extra for planetarium shows and iWerks films. 600 E. Washington St. (602) 716-2000. Web site: *www.azscience.org/* (#14, C-3, downtown)

PHOENIX MUSEUM OF HISTORY: It zeroes in on the history of Phoenix from prehistoric times to the 1930s. You'll see an interesting printing press exhibit and one of the state's oldest mining locomotives. And you can send a message by Morse code and pump water from a well, which nobody does much any more. Admission fee. 105 N. Fifth St. (602) 253-2734. (#24, C-3, downtown)

The attractions listed so far are within walking distance of one another. To visit the following sites, you'll need transportation other than your feet.

PHOENIX CENTRAL LIBRARY: It took 100,000 pounds of copper — the equivalent of 17.5 million pennies but costing only about 1/100 as much — to sheath this building. The shade sails on the north windows were crafted by Maine sail makers. They deflect heat and glare during the oh-so-hot summers, yet let visitors have a view of the city and the mountains. Computerized louvers on south windows move throughout the day, letting in light but closing out heat. The reading room is said to be the largest in North America, bigger than those of New York Public Library and the Library of Congress. 1221 N. Central Ave. (602) 262-4636. (#20, B-3, downtown)

MARGARET T. HANCE PARK: Adjoining the library, this 29-acre facility features a Japanese garden, celebrating the fact that one of Phoenix's sister cities is Hemeji, Japan. The park commonly is called Deck Park because it sits atop the capacious tunnel that spurts freeway traffic through the heart of the downtown district. 1134 N. Central Ave. (602) 534-2404.

PHOENIX ART MUSEUM: The museum houses more than 16,000 pieces, from Renaissance to contemporary Southwest to Asian and Latin American art. Members of the Cowboy Artists of America exhibit here each fall. Marvel at the Thorne miniature rooms — 21 tiny but immaculately authentic American and European interiors created by Narcissa Thorne on the scale of 1:12 (1 inch in the model equals 1 foot in real life). Kids will enjoy ArtWorks, the interactive, "please touch!" gallery just for them. Admission fee. 1625 N. Central Ave. (602) 257-1222. Web site: *www.phxart.org/* (#18, A-3, downtown)

PHOENIX PUBLIC ART PROGRAM: The city's public art program has commanded the attention of such journals as *Smithsonian* and *Newsweek.* You can get a map from the Phoenix Arts Commission at City Hall, (602) 262-4637. Then check out works such as the civil rights memorial at Eastlake Park, 16th and Jefferson streets; more than 35 pieces — planters, painted vessels, gazebos, seating niches — at sites on and around the Squaw Peak Parkway; and more.

TELEPHONE PIONEER MUSEUM: Some may remember when you picked up a phone and waited for a pleasant voice to say, "Number, please." Telephone memorabilia from those times and earlier are on display here, including Arizona's first phone at Yuma in 1878, Phoenix's first phone installed in 1882, and coin-operated phones. No admission charge, but open weekdays by appointment only. 20 E. Thomas Road, Suite 101. (602) 630-2060. (#28, A-3, downtown)

ARIZONA HALL OF FAME: The old Carnegie Library, Phoenix's first library now restored and illustrating some of the colorful state and local past. Like the story of Fred Harvey and the Harvey Girls; "Healers,

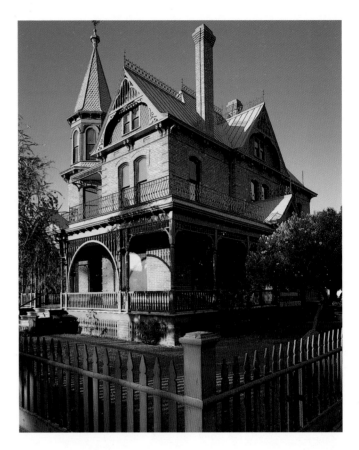

Hucksters, and Heroes" — how medicine was practiced in territorial days (if somebody operated on you, it was probably to amputate something); and "Who's Minding the Store?" — a tribute to the pioneer Jewish merchants of early Phoenix. No admission charge. 1101 W. Washington St. (602) 255-2110. (#3, C-2, downtown)

STATE CAPITOL MUSEUM: The capitol was constructed in 1899 when Arizona was a territory. The copper covering the dome — 15 tons of it — was donated by

(OPPOSITE PAGE, ABOVE) *The Arizona Center features shops and restaurants as well as fountains, gardens, and walkways.* TOM BEAN
(OPPOSITE PAGE, BELOW) *Modern fountains at Phoenix Civic Plaza frame St. Mary's Basilica, Phoenix's oldest church still in use.* JERRY SIEVE
(ABOVE) *Rosson House is a major attraction at Heritage Square.* GEORGE STOCKING
(LEFT) *Margaret T. Hance Park, adjacent to the Phoenix Public Library, is built on a deck over a freeway.* DAVID H. SMITH

ARIZONA MINING & MINERAL MUSEUM: We're a big copper-producing state, and so there are tools, machinery, and colorful samples here from Arizona's copper mines, including an eight-foot piece of native copper and an 1882 baby-gauge steam locomotive from the huge open pit at Morenci. The museum displays more than 3,000 minerals, a 206-pound meteorite chunk from Meteor Crater, and rocks from the first moon landing. No admission charge. 1502 W. Washington St. (602) 255-3791. Web site: *www.admmr.state.az.us/* (#4, C-2, downtown)

PIONEER AND MILITARY MEMORIAL PARK: Buried here is legendary Jacob Waltz, who supposedly found scads of gold in what came to be known as the Lost Dutchman Mine but died without revealing its exact spot in the Superstition Mountains. Also here are John Tabor Alsap, Phoenix's first mayor; Capt. William A. Hancock (an honorary title — lieutenant was his highest rank in the Civil War), who laid out the first Phoenix townsite; and Indian fighter King S. Woolsey. Darrell Duppa, who named Phoenix, was buried here but was reburied at Greenwood Cemetery, not far away. The park's monument to Waltz depicts Weaver's Needle and other landmarks in the Superstitions. 15th Avenue and Jefferson Street. (602) 262-6412. (#26, C-2, downtown)

the state's huge copper industry. All of the original capitol is now a museum, including the old governor's office and the House and Senate chambers. Atop the building stands Winged Victory — a statue holding a torch in her right hand and the laurel wreath of victory in her left. No admission charge. 1700 W. Washington St. (602) 542-4675 or 542-4581. (#6, C-2, downtown)

WESLEY BOLIN MEMORIAL PLAZA: The capitol plaza named for a former secretary of state and governor. Memorials and monuments here honor figures such as Father Eusebio Kino, the gutsy Jesuit missionary who came to Arizona in the 1690s and established the San Xavier Mission in Tucson; the Bushmasters, an Arizona unit in World War II that General Douglas MacArthur described as "the greatest fighting combat team ever deployed for battle"; Phoenix flyer Frank Luke, who shot down more German reconnaissance balloons than anyone else in WW I; and the veterans of Korea, Vietnam, and Desert Storm. You'll also see the signal mast and anchor from the battleship *USS Arizona*, which sank at Pearl Harbor. (#30, C-2, downtown)

(OPPOSITE PAGE, ABOVE) *The old copper-roofed State Capitol building, now a museum, houses various exhibits depicting aspects of Arizona's history.* (OPPOSITE PAGE, BELOW) *Phoenix Mystery Castle displays an eclectic array of oddities.* BOTH BY RICHARD MAACK
(BELOW, RIGHT) *A costumed guide demonstrates frontier skills in the working blacksmith shop at the Pioneer Arizona Living History Museum.* BRAD MELTON

MYSTERY CASTLE: This eccentric edifice lies straight south of downtown Phoenix in South Mountain Park's foothills. It was built by Boyce Gulley, a health refugee from Seattle. "Please, Daddy, build me a big castle some day that I can live in," said his daughter, Mary Lou. And he did. It took 16 years, starting in 1929, and very little money, because Gulley didn't have much. The 18 rooms and 13 fireplaces came from a startling mix of oddities: a ceiling made of the sides of boxcars and old railroad ties; a bar fashioned from a Conestoga wagon; chairs from cactus skeletons. Mary Lou stays on the premises and guides visitors. Admission fee (reservations required). Closed July through September. 800 E. Mineral Road, South Mountain Park. (602) 268-1581. (#61, K-7)

WILDLIFE WORLD ZOO: A 45-acre, privately-run collection that calls itself Arizona's largest assemblage of exotic animals. You can wander among carnivores such as lions and Bengal tigers; hoofed animals such as rhinos, giraffes, and zebras; marsupials such as kangaroos and wallabies; primates such as monkeys, gibbons, and lemurs; and birds, reptiles, and fish. Admission fee. 16501 W. Northern Ave. (623) 935-9453. (#117, G-2)

GLENDALE: Once a little farm town — kind of square, kind of funky, very quiet — just west of Phoenix, it's much bigger now, but still a little square and a little funky. Glendale's thing is antiques, and you can roam — on foot or by trolley if you want to park the car — downtown Glendale's Old Towne Glendale and historic Catlin Court shopping districts. Catlin Court's restored bungalows offer all manner of antiques, crafts, folk art, and collectibles like one-of-a-kind beads and eclectic '50s kitsch. There are more than 90 such antique stores, specialty shops and restaurants. There are quaint tea rooms and a chocolate factory that offers tours. Take it all in with Glendale's holiday evening antique walk, starting the day after Thanksgiving and running Thursday to Saturday through December. Another arts, crafts, and collectibles event, the Market at Murphy Park, runs Saturdays, October through May; call (623) 435-0556 for specifics on both events and trolley information. Glendale offers its Old Time Watermelon Festival in June, the Front Porch Festival in September, and April's Jazz and Blues Festival. Glimpse more of the city's picturesque past at Sahuaro Ranch, a century-old ranch and one of the Valley's oldest homesteads — the only one with a lavish

rose garden and live peacocks strolling the grounds. Admission fee. 59th and Mountain View avenues. For ranch tour and event information, call (623) 939-5782.

LUKE AIR FORCE BASE: The largest fighter training base in the western world, the base west of Glendale offers tours and hosts an annual air show — call (623) 856-5853. (G-2)

PIONEER ARIZONA LIVING HISTORY MUSEUM: Frontier Arizona comes alive with demonstrations of skills necessary to life back then. Reconstructed buildings

include a working blacksmith shop, a sheriff's office and jail, and Spanish Colonial houses. Reviving some Old West entertainment, the Whiskey-Road-to-Ruin Saloon has a cherry bar that was shipped by boat around Cape Horn, and the opera house hosts melodramas. Costumed guides show how to quilt and how to make ice cream. Admission fee. Closed September for maintenance. North of Phoenix, take Exit 255 (Pioneer Road) off Interstate 17. (623) 465-1052. (#78, B-6)

DEER VALLEY ROCK ART CENTER: There are some 1,500 ancient Indian petroglyphs to be seen. Arizona State University's department of anthropology operates the center. Admission fee. 3711 W. Deer Valley Road. (623) 582-8007. (#31, D-6) ◪

When You Go

Greater Phoenix Convention & Visitors Bureau: (602) 252-5588 or (877) 225-5749. *www.phoenixcvb.com/*

Phoenix Parks and Recreation: (602) 262-6861.

Glendale: city switchboard, (623) 930-2000; special events hotline, (623) 930-2299. Glendale Chamber of Commerce, (623) 937-4754 or (800) 437-8669.

Web Sites: For information about attractions and events. *www.arizonaguide.com/*

www.ci.phoenix.az.us/

www.ci.glendale.az.us/

tour.glendaleaz.org/

Getting Acquainted *with the* East Valley

FOCUSING ON THE AREA'S UNIQUENESS

by Joe Stocker

Watch a cheetah chase a target as if it were prey . . . view a garden of desert plants from around the world . . . stroll along a turn-of-the-century-style street . . . inspect century-old fire trucks . . . see historic railroad engines and cars . . . view art of almost any genre . . . practice orienteering . . . visit a farmers' market.

Zoos, museums, and other attractions in east Phoenix and neighboring communities offer a panoply of seeing and doing. These attractions aren't as concentrated as those in the heart of the city. You may have needed a car to see those; you'll certainly need a car to see these. Many listings include a site number and grid coordinates corresponding to the foldout map following Page 130.

Overview: This is the second of four chapters dealing primarily with the most popular attractions in an area commonly called the Valley of the Sun. Here, we focus on sight-seeing and attractions in east Phoenix — primarily in and around Papago Park — and in Tempe, Mesa, Scottsdale, Fountain Hills, Gilbert, and Chandler. Many of the attractions showcase the history, culture, lifestyles, and vegetation of Arizona and the Southwest. Chapter 17 covers downtown Phoenix and areas north, west, and south of the core. The following chapter deals with enjoying the outdoors in an urban area.

EAST PHOENIX

PAPAGO PARK: This 1,200-acre preserve has facilities for picnicking and cookouts, archery, baseball, softball, volleyball, fishing, golf, hiking, biking, and orienteering. Papago Park also has the Hole in the Rock, a natural geologic formation. Weather carved what was once a massive granite mountain 1.7 billion years ago into buttes with openings called windows, or tafoni. Van Buren Street and Galvin Parkway. (602) 256-3220 or 262-4599. (#68, H-9)

DESERT BOTANICAL GARDEN: At Papago Park, a hundred thousand visitors a year tour this 145-acre collection of cactuses, succulents, and desert flowers from arid lands worldwide. There are more than 4,000 species and 10,000 plants, and jackrabbits, squirrels, quail, and desert tortoises live among them. In early spring, there's an explosion of color as the desert wildflowers bloom. Visit the experimental Desert House, devoted to learning to live comfortably in the desert while conserving natural resources. Admission fee. 1201 N. Galvin Parkway. (602) 941-1225. Web site: *www.dbg.org/* (#32, H-9)

PHOENIX ZOO: It spreads over 125 acres in Papago Park. Four trails lead visitors through themed experiences. The trails focus on Arizona, Africa, the Tropics, and children's interests. Along the way you'll see 1,300 animals, including the endangered spectacled bear of the South American Andes and the Arabian oryx. The zoo helped save the oryx from extinction by establishing a captive breeding program for exotic antelope. In all, more than 150 endangered species live at the zoo.

At the zoo's Harmony Farm, children and their families can learn the relationships among people, plants, and animals. Families, too, will delight when the zoo dazzles with Christmas lights strung throughout the

(OPPOSITE PAGE) *Although not open to the public, Tovrea Castle is an east Phoenix landmark.* RICHARD MAACK (TOP) *A child rides the 50-year-old restored carousel at McCormick-Stillman Railroad Park in Scottsdale.* (ABOVE) *Students pore over an interpretive station at the Desert Botanical Garden, which has thousands of plants with animals living among them.* BOTH BY DAVID H. SMITH

riverbed had many naysayers, but the City of Tempe made it happen. Stroll, skate, or bike along wide paths through desert plants and ceramic murals. Rent a watercraft, bring your own (boating permit required), or take an excursion cruise. For information, visit the operations center at the south end of the Red River Music Hall parking lot, southwest corner of Mill Avenue and Curry Road. (480) 350-8625. (J-9) Web site: *www.tempe.gov/rio/*

OLD TOWN TEMPE: Along Mill Avenue, First Street to University Drive, old buildings have been cannily preserved and transformed into an eclectic shopping, eating, and strolling neighborhood just off the Arizona State University campus. It's a fun place, frequented by locals, students, and visitors. When there's something to celebrate, Tempe does it along Mill Avenue. No fewer than seven annual festivals are held there, including the Fiesta Bowl block party. Twice a year the Festival of the Arts hosts artists and craftspeople who beckon you to inspect (and, of course, buy) their wares. (J-9)

TEMPE ARTS CENTER: As you come off the bridge, you'll see the center on your right, in Tempe Beach Park. The center features contemporary work, much of it by local artists, and sponsors community art events. Mill Avenue and First Street. (480) 968-0888. (#101, J-9)

WALKING ART TOUR: If it's art you're interested in, take downtown Tempe's eight-block walking tour of public art. Pick up a map and brochure at the Tempe Convention and Visitors Bureau, 51 W. Third St., and take a look at such things as a sidewalk hopscotch board, 13 artistic light fixtures, a metal gateway to a sculpture garden, and a larger-than-life bronze sculpture of Tempe's founder, Charles Trumbull Hayden.

complex, which stays open into the evening for the spectacle. Admission fee. 455 N. Galvin Parkway. (602) 273-1341. Web site: *www.phoenixzoo.org/* (#77, H-9)

ARIZONA MILITARY MUSEUM: Weapons, paintings, historical photos, and a military helicopter are among the displays recalling Arizona's military history dating back centuries to the Spanish conquistadors. 5636 E. McDowell Road. (602) 267-2676. (#6, H-8)

HALL OF FLAME: In this museum of fire fighting, you'll see more than 90 pieces of fire-fighting apparatus dating back to 1725: a 1915 American La France fire engine that kids can climb on; a pumper used to fight the 1871 Chicago fire; hook and ladder wagons from the 18th and 19th centuries; and Phoenix's original computerized alarm system, said to be the first in the United States. Admission fee. 6101 E. Van Buren St. (602) 275-3473. (#49, H-9)

SHEMER ART CENTER: Exhibits by local and national artists are showcased in this Santa Fe-style house dating to the 1920s in Phoenix's nicely-turned-out Arcadia section. 5005 E. Camelback. (602) 262-4727. (#92, G-8)

TEMPE

Enter this university city by way of the Mill Avenue bridge over the Salt River.

TEMPE TOWN LAKE: A man-made lake in a dry

ARIZONA HISTORICAL SOCIETY MUSEUM: The state's oldest such institution, with branches in Tempe, Tucson, Yuma, and Flagstaff. The one in Tempe, known also as the Marley Center, features imaginatively designed displays and a video showing what made the Salt River Valley the agricultural and economic cornucopia that it is. 1300 N. College Ave. (480) 929-0292. (#5, H-9)

SALT RIVER PROJECT HISTORY CENTER: A dramatic map displayed in the lobby outside the museum shows today's irrigation canals overlaid on the original system constructed by the ancient Hohokam. Housed in headquarters of the Salt River Project, the center showcases SRP's water management responsibilities as prime supplier of surface water and one of two providers of electricity to metropolitan Phoenix. A self-guided tour takes 30 to 40 minutes. 1521 E. Project Drive, across the street from the Hall of Flame (Phoenix). (602) 236-2208. (H-9)

ARIZONA STATE UNIVERSITY

ASU's main campus in Tempe offers a wide range of cultural and educational sites. Sun Devil Stadium hosts professional and ASU football, plus the Fiesta Bowl.

VISITORS CENTER: Get a campus map and other information here. Students on staff can answer questions, point out interesting sights, and give you tips about the Tempe area. 826 E. Apache Boulevard at Rural Road. (480) 965-0100. Web site: *www.asu.edu/*

GAMMAGE AUDITORIUM: This desert-tinted circular building with globe-illuminated ramps and sculpted contour curtains was the last public structure designed by Frank Lloyd Wright. Major stage and musical productions held here. (480) 965-5062, 965-3434. (#47, J-9)

NELSON FINE ARTS CENTER: A very modern building of gray-purple stucco containing a playhouse, dance laboratory, and art galleries. Houses half of ASU's

TEMPE HISTORICAL MUSEUM: Charles Trumbull Hayden settled at a crossing of the Salt River in 1871 and built a flour mill, which still stands. Exhibits tell the story of Hayden, his flour mill, the founding of Tempe, and the diversion of the Salt River, which supplied water to this desert valley. Hayden's son, Senator Carl T. Hayden, was at the time of his death in 1972 Congress' longest-serving member. Admission fee. 809 E. Southern Ave. (480) 350-5100; recording, 350-5125. (#103, J-9)

PETERSEN HOUSE MUSEUM: This Queen Anne-style Victorian pink lovely from 1892 is listed in the National Register of Historic Places. Danish immigrant Niels Petersen built it to anchor his 160-acre ranch. Now it anchors a small park with picnic area and playground. The interior includes hand-stenciled wallpaper and other ornate touches. Donation requested. 1414 W. Southern Ave. at Priest Drive. (480) 350-5151. (#72, J-8)

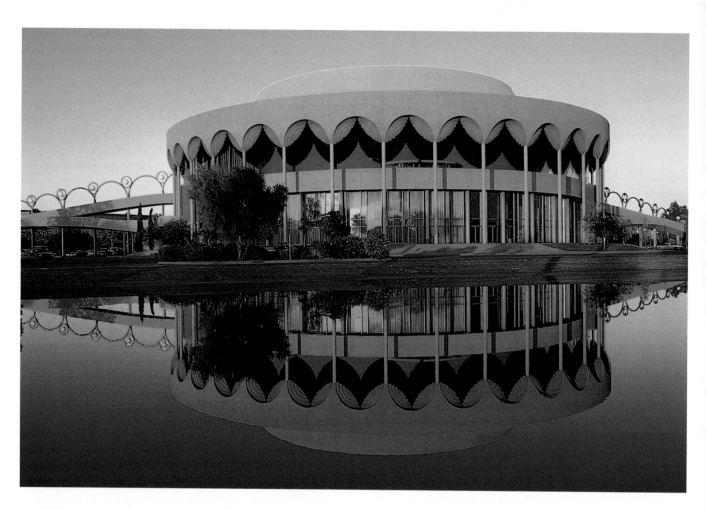

art holdings; the other half is at Matthews Center, farther northeast on the campus. (480) 965-0100. (#63, J-9)

PHYSICAL SCIENCES BUILDING: See one of the world's outstanding collections of meteorites and the campus planetarium, too. (480) 965-0100.

LIFE SCIENCES CENTER: Live desert denizens such as rattlesnakes and Gila monsters safely displayed here, along with plants and fossil collections. (480) 965-0100.

SCOTTSDALE

A Civil War veteran and later Army chaplain, Winfield Scott bought desert land here in 1888 to grow citrus, sweet potatoes, and peanuts. From that beginning came Scottsdale, which likes to call itself "the West's most Western town." But its "Westernness" has yielded somewhat to glitz and posh. The city has more five-star resorts than any other U.S. city. Art galleries literally line the downtown streets, and there's an art walk on Thursday evenings during which patrons meet the artists and see their works. City boosters like to tell you that you can play golf on any of the more than 180 golf courses here and around the Valley.

You can shop until you drop in upscale malls like the Italian-styled Borgata and Scottsdale Fashion Square, but you won't need to drive. Ollie the Trolley gets you around the heart of Scottsdale, stopping at resorts, malls, and

(ABOVE) *Concerts and theater productions are among the performances at ASU's Grady Gammage Auditorium, designed by Frank Lloyd Wright.* JAMES TALLON
(OPPOSITE PAGE, ABOVE) *Scottsdale Fashion Square is one of many upscale shopping malls in the city.* DAVID H. SMITH
(OPPOSITE PAGE, BELOW) *Visitors enjoy a ride on a miniature steam-engine train at McCormick-Stillman Railroad Park in Scottsdale. The city park also displays full-size engines and train cars.* DAVID H. SMITH

entertainment and dining places. Riding Ollie is free from mid-October to May, but it doesn't run during the summer. For a schedule, call (480) 970-8130.

SCOTTSDALE CIVIC CENTER MALL: This is a manicured and be-flowered promenade with sculpture, fountains, and gardens. Brick sidewalks link City Hall, Civic Center Library, and Scottsdale Center for the Arts, a stage for performing and visual arts. The mall complex straddles Civic Center Boulevard south of Indian School Road, east of Scottsdale Road. Center for the Arts, (480) 994-2787. (#88, H-9)

SCOTTSDALE HISTORICAL MUSEUM: Housed in the original Scottsdale Grammar School (the Little Red Schoolhouse) built in 1909, it features permanent and traveling exhibits focusing on the history of Scottsdale and the Salt River Valley. 7333 E. Scottsdale Mall (100 yards east of the intersection of Brown and Main Streets in Old Town Scottsdale). Open Wednesday through Sunday, September through June; closed July and August. No admission charge. (480) 945-4499. (#90, G-9)

THE GREENBELT (INDIAN BEND WASH): Extending 7.5 miles from Indian Bend Road almost to the Salt River, the strip functions as flood control but provides a wide range of recreational facilities. One greenbelt element, 60-acre Eldorado Park, features ramadas, five picnic areas, three lighted softball fields, a soccer field, a basketball court, a sand volleyball court, an outdoor amphitheater, swimming pool, two lakes (if older than 14, you must have a valid fishing license from Arizona Game and Fish Department), two playgrounds, a 5K course, horseshoe courts, and an inline-skating area. 2311 N. Miller Road at Oak St. (480) 994-2483.

MCCORMICK-STILLMAN RAILROAD PARK: First, the viewing. On display are steam and diesel engines, a Pullman car that carried four presidents — Herbert Hoover, Franklin Roosevelt, Harry Truman, and Dwight Eisenhower — as they whistle-stopped during election campaigns in the 1940s and '50s, a couple of old depots, a French Forty and Eight boxcar that carried troops and pack animals in World War I, and an arboretum. Now, the riding. You and the kids can ride around the park on a five-twelfths-scale train. Park admission is free, but there are ride fares. 7301 E. Indian Bend Road. (480) 312-2312.

BUFFALO MUSEUM OF AMERICA: This privately owned museum heralds — you might have guessed by now — the buffalo. On display is a rifle said to have been used by Buffalo Bill. Admission fee. 10261 N. Scottsdale Road. (480) 951-1022. (#16, F-9)

SYLVIA PLOTKIN JUDAICA MUSEUM: Housed in the cultural wing of Temple Beth Israel's architecturally striking complex, the Southwest's only museum of Judaica features a 1,000-piece collection rotated seasonally, three temporary exhibits a year, and various special events. Docents give guided tours. A reconstructed Tunisian synagogue occupies one alcove in the museum, and a 20,000-volume library and video collection provide a one-of-a-kind resource on Jewish culture.

(LEFT) *Taliesin West is an accredited architectural school and the winter home of the Taliesin Fellowship, founded by Frank Lloyd Wright.* DAVID H. SMITH
(RIGHT) *Millennium and Calvin lounge together at the Out of Africa Wildlife Park.* RICHARD MAACK
(BELOW) *Visitors watch a wild west reenactment at Rawhide, a western theme park.* JIM MARSHALL

Donation requested. Open Tuesday through Friday. 10460 N. 56th St. at Shea Boulevard. (480) 951-0323.

TALIESIN WEST: Famed architect Frank Lloyd Wright's winter headquarters and architectural school on the western slopes of the McDowell Mountains, the campus is a national historic landmark. It's pure Frank Lloyd Wright, with angular rock and redwood seemingly growing out of the thorny desert landscape. Still an active school, Taliesin West offers several guided tour options, most not needing reservations. Admission fee. Northeast Scottsdale, Cactus Road and Frank Lloyd Wright Boulevard (114th Street). Recorded tour information, (480) 860-8810. Web site: *www.franklloydwright.org/* (#99, F-10)

FLEISCHER MUSEUM: The passion here is American Impressionism (California School), emphasizing sunlight and brilliantly hued landscapes, and Soviet and Russian art. Besides the 300 paintings (about one-third shown at a time), don't miss the sculpture garden. Open daily. No admission charge. Call ahead to request a guided tour. The Perimeter Center, Bell and Pima roads. (480) 585-3108. Web site: *www.fleischer.org/*

OUT OF AFRICA WILDLIFE PARK: Normally, big cats — lions, tigers, leopards — would not get along with each other. But they do at this privately operated park where you can view them and many other wild creatures, handle and otherwise interact with animals, and watch shows such as one in which the big cats and handlers frolic in a pool. Admission fee. 9736 N. Ft. McDowell Road. Take State Route 87 (Beeline Highway) two miles north of Shea Boulevard and turn right onto Fort McDowell Road. (480) 837-7779. (#66, F-13)

RAWHIDE: Commercial but fun, this re-creation of an 1880s Western town has stagecoach and burro rides, gold panning, staged frontier gun battles, a petting zoo, and vagrant sheep on the streets. 23023 N. Scottsdale Road. (480) 502-1880 or (800) 527-1880. (#81, D-9)

MESA

In 1878, 80 Mormon pioneers from Utah and Idaho settled and started farming on a mesa overlooking the Salt River. The town's streets were made really wide, as legend has it, so 20-mule teams could negotiate U-turns.

MESA SOUTHWEST MUSEUM: Animated dinosaurs roar as visitors wander through simulations of caves, Hohokam dwellings, and prehistoric oceans. View artifacts from the various cultures that first populated the Valley, and puzzle over the lost meaning of Hohokam petroglyphs (rock art). Recently expanded, the museum added a gem and mineral hall, a meteorite exhibit, and Dinosaur Mountain — a monumental display of life, dinosaur and otherwise, in prehistoric Arizona. Admission fee. Downtown at First and Macdonald streets. (480) 644-2230. (#59, J-10)

ARIZONA MUSEUM FOR YOUTH: Living by its slogan, "An art museum you can kid around in!," the museum brings in traveling exhibits and sponsors hands-on

programs (led by professional artists) to encourage creativity and art appreciation in young people. Admission fee. 35 N. Robson St. (480) 644-2467. (#8, J-10)

MESA ARTS CENTER: The center hosts contemporary art exhibits and concerts and sponsors workshops and other programs in the visual and performing arts. 155 N. Center. (480) 644-2242. (#41, J-10)

SIRRINE HOUSE: See a 1906 washing machine and other period antiques and collectibles in a Victorian-style house built in 1896 by pioneer Joel Sirrine. Open weekends, October through March. No charge. 160 N. Center St. in downtown Mesa. (480) 644-2760. (J-10)

ARIZONA TEMPLE: Except for an inner sanctum for Mormons only, the temple is open to visitors year-round. Call for Christmas concert and Easter pageant schedule. 525 E. Main St. Visitors center, (480) 964-7164.

PARK OF THE CANALS: Ancient remnants of the Hohokam canals are preserved here, which the National Geographic Society has called an important prehistoric site. Enjoy a stroll through the desert botanical garden, too. 1710 N. Horne St. Mesa Parks, (480) 644-2351.

MESA HISTORICAL MUSEUM: A nostalgic look at Mesa's hardy pioneer families and the city's early farming roots, set in the last remaining turn-of-the-century Mesa schoolhouse. Donations accepted. 2345 N. Horne St. (480) 835-7358.

CONFEDERATE AIR FORCE MUSEUM: The Arizona Wing of this organization displays war planes — mostly from World War II — and related memorabilia. Admission fee. Falcon Field at McKellips and Greenfield roads. (480) 924-1940. (30, H-12)

CHAMPLIN FIGHTER AIRCRAFT MUSEUM: Three hangars hold a superb collection of more than 30 fighter planes in flying condition from all the major 20th-century wars. Exhibits include combat footage and flyers' memorabilia. While the museum changed hands recently, don't expect its location to change any time soon. Admission fee. Falcon Field, off McKellips Road, east of Greenfield Road. (480) 830-4540. (#25, H-12)

GILBERT

Gilbert might be mistaken for a newer East Valley community, but its rustic Main Street hints at its farming roots that date back to the early 1900s.

GILBERT HISTORICAL MUSEUM: Glimpse Gilbert's past — from now back to prehistory — through the exhibits in this quaint old schoolhouse. Open Tuesday and Saturday, October through May. No admission charge. 10 S. Gilbert Rd. (480) 926-1577.

FARMERS' MARKET: Find farm-fresh produce and craft items here Saturday mornings year-round. At the park by the Gilbert Historical Museum. (602) 848-1234.

RIPARIAN PRESERVES: Part of Gilbert's water reclamation effort, these two parks let you stroll through wetland and desert habitats, some of which are rapidly disappearing in the wild. No admission fee, but program fee for scheduled astronomy and nocturnal wildlife tours. The Audubon Society has spotted 140 different bird species here. The preserve at Water Ranch (Greenfield and Guadalupe roads) has 4.5 miles of trails where you can birdwatch, stroll, or bike on your own and a small lake open for fishing (subject to local regulations). The Neely Ranch site, on Cooper Road between Guadalupe and Elliot roads, has a butterfly and hummingbird garden. (480) 503-6744. (#85, K-12)

(OPPOSITE PAGE, ABOVE) *Champlin Fighter Museum specializes in planes like these propeller models.* JEFF KIDA
(OPPOSITE PAGE, BELOW) *Llamas also race at the ostrich festival held in Chandler.* EDWARD McCAIN
(LEFT) *The Arizona Temple glows at Christmas.* DEBS METZONG

CHANDLER

With high-tech plants of companies like Motorola and Allied Signal, Chandler is part of what boosters call the "Silicon Desert." Town founder Dr. A.B. Chandler raised ostriches, and Chandler's whimsical ostrich festival and races in March attract thousands.

FARMERS' MARKET: Fresh produce and other items sold Thursday afternoons (except in summer) at the outdoor market. At Chandler Park, Boston Street and Arizona Avenue. (480) 782-3045.

CHANDLER CENTER FOR THE ARTS: A major investment in the cultural arts, the turntable auditorium seats 1,560, with two rear seating sections that can rotate to face smaller stages. Arizona Avenue at Chandler Boulevard. Box office, (480) 782-2680. (#26, L-10)

VISION GALLERY: Hosts collections from local artists and free Kidz Art workshops for children. Chandler Park, 80 South San Marcos Place. (480) 917-6859. (L-10)

XERISCAPE DEMONSTRATION GARDEN: Shows the beauty and practicality of low-water-use landscaping. Erie Street and Arrowhead Drive. (480) 782-3580.

ARIZONA RAILWAY MUSEUM: Resembling a train depot, the museum has vintage railroad cars and state railroad archives. 399 N. Delaware Street. Open weekends. Donations requested. (480) 821-1108. (L-10) ⬇

When You Go

Chandler Chamber of Commerce: (480) 963-4571.

Gilbert Chamber of Commerce: (480) 892-0056.

Information on Arizona farmers' markets: USDA state farmers' market representative, (602) 542-0971. www.ams.usda.gov/farmersmarkets/states/arizona.htm/

Mesa Convention & Visitors Bureau: (480) 827-4700 or (800) 283-6372. www.mesacvb.com/

Mill Avenue Merchants Association: Tempe. (480) 967-4877.

Greater Phoenix Convention & Visitors Bureau: (602) 252-5588 or (877) 225-5749. www.phoenixcvb.com/

Scottsdale Chamber of Commerce: (480) 945-8481.

Tempe Chamber of Commerce: (480) 967-7891.

Tempe Convention & Visitors Bureau: (480) 894-8158.

The Valley's Urban Outdoors

STAYING CLOSE WHILE YOU GET OUT

by Joe Stocker

Let's begin exploring the urban outdoors by going to Apache Junction, on the far east side of the Valley. From there, we'll follow the Apache Trail, a marvelous backroad drive (a passenger car can readily make the trip) through richly vegetated Sonoran Desert. The venture along the Salt River and some of its lakes takes you past a re-created mining town, state park, national forest, and the legendary Superstition Mountains.

Apache Trail (State Route 88) was hacked through the mountains, canyons, and desert in the early 1900s to bring supplies for building Theodore Roosevelt Dam. When he came for the dam's dedication, Roosevelt defined the Apache Trail as "the most sublimely beautiful panorama nature has ever created."

Even before the road, there was a trail. Two ancient cultures, the Hohokam and the Salado, flourished in this area. In the mid- and late-1800s, Apaches lived there.

Many miners roamed over the Superstitions in search of wealth. Some found it; others met death. One of them, Jacob Waltz, claimed to have found an immensely rich mine, but died without revealing its exact location. His cryptic directions were to look where the shadow of Weavers Needle falls at 4 P.M. The shadow, of course, falls in a different line each day of the year. With his death was born the legend of the Lost Dutchman Mine.

The Apache Trail begins east of Phoenix in Apache Junction. From U.S. Route 60, take Idaho Road north to University Drive/Superstition Boulevard. From this junction, Idaho Road becomes the Apache Trail/State Route 88, angling to the right (east). From Apache Junction to Roosevelt Dam is about 42 miles on Apache Trail, but since about half is unpaved, allow extra driving time. Here are some points along way:

GOLDFIELD: Gold made this place a boomtown in the late 1800s. Then the place was abandoned. What you see today is a re-creation. It has an underground mine to walk through, weathered buildings, and a museum. The marked turnoff is about four miles from the start of Apache Trail/State 88. Admission fee. (480) 983-0333.

LOST DUTCHMAN STATE PARK: The entrance is a mile north of Goldfield. Located at the base of the Superstition Mountains, the park contains several hiking and nature trails. As you enter, ask at the ranger station for a trail guide. The Discovery Trail is posted with signs identifying plants and relating highlights of the area's natural history. You'll have a great view of the Superstitions. Along its 0.3-mile length is a pond that attracts birds and

Overview: This, the third chapter on attractions in the Salt River Valley, or the Valley of the Sun, focuses on enjoying the "urban outdoors." Imagine being on a mountain trail, with wildflowers and saguaro, barrel, and other cactuses all around you. Perhaps a stream, too. Birds flutter about. Some bicycle riders strain to pedal up a nearby hill. Hikers and their dog make their way across a ridge. Only the whisper of a breeze breaks the silence. Ah, this is a place to relax and enjoy nature, and you can do so in the midst of the metropolitan area and along its edges. The Tonto National Forest and state, regional, and city parks maintain these urban sanctuaries. When appropriate, descriptions list a site number and grid coordinates corresponding with the foldout map following Page 130. The sites are listed in accordance with their locations — beginning with east areas and moving to north, west, and south areas.

(OPPOSITE PAGE) *A monsoon strikes along the Apache Trail in the Superstition Mountains.* GEORGE STOCKING
(TOP) *A jogger makes her way over a trail on Camelback Mountain, in the heart of Phoenix.* PETER NOEBELS
(RIGHT) *Nature lovers will enjoy a stroll in Lost Dutchman State Park, here decorated with Mexican gold poppies and lupine. The rugged butte is the western end of the Superstition Mountains.* BOB & SUZANNE CLEMENZ

The Valley's Urban Outdoors 147

other critters. A second nature trail is the Native Plant Trail. Hiking the Siphon Draw Trail (a 2.2-mile round trip) is more strenuous, but the reward is a fantastic view of the mountains. Vehicle entry fee. (480) 982-4485.

TONTO NATIONAL FOREST: About a mile past the park, the Apache Trail comes to Forest Service Road 87 on the right. About a mile onto this dirt road, you'll reach First Water Trailhead, starting point for several hiking and horse trails into the heart of the Superstition Mountains. The Mesa Ranger Station has maps and detailed information. Vehicle entry fee. (480) 610-3300.

CANYON LAKE AND BEYOND: Just past Milepost 208 is the turnoff to Canyon Lake, which has sandy beaches on one side and steep canyon walls on the other. You can try warm-water fishing, boating, skiing, camping,

even a sternwheeler cruise. Across the road from the marina is Boulder Canyon Trailhead. If you're up to some steep and rocky terrain, the mile-long opening climb up La Barge Canyon's eastern wall reaches a view of the Superstitions and Four Peaks (the full trail is 7.3 miles one way). Fees for some facilities. Marina, (602) 944-6504. Mesa Ranger District, (480) 610-3300.

At this point you are about a fourth of the way to Roosevelt dam and lake, and the pavement's about to end. Ahead a mile or so lies the minute community of Tortilla Flat, with a restaurant and souvenir shops; a scenic, steep, narrow, and winding passage over Fish Creek Hill; Apache Lake; and then Roosevelt dam and lake.

Now, let's explore more of the east Salt River Valley.

(ABOVE) *The Four Peaks area of the Tonto National Forest makes demands on hikers.* JERRY JACKA
(LEFT) *A steep canyon wall forms one side of Canyon Lake.* STEVE BRUNO
(OPPOSITE PAGE, LEFT) *Waterskiers favor Saguaro Lake on the Salt River east of Phoenix.* TOM JOHNSON
(OPPOSITE PAGE, RIGHT) *A fisherman on the trout-stocked Salt River just below Saguaro Lake has the spot to himself.* JERRY JACKA

USERY MOUNTAIN RECREATION AREA: The name comes from King Usery, a homegrown desperado and horse thief who lived around these parts during the late 1800s. Many trails, ranging from 0.2 to about seven miles long, take you through great desert vegetation and offer sensational views of the Superstitions. The 2.9-mile loop of Blevins Trail is popular with novice mountain bikers. Horseback riders especially enjoy this area, with its facilities for picnicking, camping, and archery. Vehicle entry fee. From U.S. Route 60, take Ellsworth Road north until it turns into Usery Pass Road; the park entrance is past McDowell Road. (480) 984-0032 or Maricopa County Parks Department, (602) 506-2930.

SAGUARO LAKE: The four Salt River lakes are, beginning upstream, Roosevelt, Apache, Canyon and Saguaro. Like Canyon Lake, Saguaro offers boat rentals, lake cruises, a restaurant, and other water sports facilities. When fishing's good, you can catch largemouth and yellow bass, blue gill, walleye, and channel catfish. The most accessible of the lakes, Saguaro fills up fast on weekends. Reach it from the Beeline Highway/State Route 87, Power Road/Bush Highway, or Usery Pass Road. Marina, (480) 986-5546. Boat rentals, (480) 986-0969.

SALT RIVER TUBING: From about April or May through October, throngs of people float down the river on inner tubes. Headquarters for "tubing" the river are at Salt River Recreation and Tubing, Inc., in the Tonto National Forest. You park there, rent tubes, and ride a shuttle to up-river access points. Take munchies and beverages (no glass containers allowed). Wear shady headgear and sneakers to protect your feet from the river rocks. From U.S. 60, take Power Road north to where it becomes Bush Highway, angling northeast until you reach Usery Pass Road. Salt River Recreation's entrance is on Usery Pass, just past the junction. (480) 984-3305.

PHON D. SUTTON RECREATION SITE: This national forest site on the Salt River offers river access, fishing, and a nature trail with signs telling you about the plants and terrain. Joggers like the essentially level, 2.3-mile trail. Fee. Mesa Ranger Station, (480) 610-3300.

MCDOWELL MOUNTAIN REGIONAL PARK: At this county park, you'll see scenic views of the McDowell Mountains. Five miles of paved roads and more than 50 miles of trails for hiking, horseback riding, and mountain biking branch through the park. Vehicle entry fee. Take Shea Boulevard east to Fountain Hills Boulevard, then go north on Fountain Hills to the entrance on McDowell Mountain Road. (480) 471-0173. (D-12)

CAVE CREEK TRAIL SYSTEM: You'll be surprised when you visit this area, used by hikers, horseback riders, and campers. The system centers on Cave Creek, which flows all year. So, you'll move through a mixture of cactus and other desert plants, plus such streamside vegetation as cottonwood trees. The trailheads and campgrounds are at Seven Springs on Forest Service Road 24. From Carefree (B-9), go east and then north on Cave Creek Road, which takes you to FR 24. The last few miles of the 17-mile drive from Carefree are unpaved and bumpy, but a sedan can make the trip readily. Tonto National Forest's Carefree Ranger Station is on Cave Creek Road at the Bartlett Lake turnoff. (480) 595-3300.

BEN AVERY SHOOTING FACILITY: Among the nation's largest shooting facilities, it offers shooting ranges (rifle, pistol, archery, and air guns) and campsites. Maricopa County Parks Department operates it with Arizona Game and Fish Department and Arizona Rifle and Pistol Association. Off Carefree Highway (the road to Lake Pleasant) west of Interstate 17. From I-17, take Exit 223. (623) 582-8313.

LAKE PLEASANT REGIONAL PARK: Like the lakes on the Salt River, Lake Pleasant supplies irrigation water to farms, so its level varies seasonally, but it's always a playground and a warm-water fishing and boating spot. Sailors like the lake's open waters, unlike the cliff-girded lakes east of Phoenix. Vehicle entry fee. From I-17, take the Carefree Highway west at Exit 223. From the northwest valley, take 99th Avenue/Lake Pleasant Road north. Ranger station, (520) 501-1710. Marina, (623) 566-3100 or (520) 501-3100. (A-4)

ADOBE DAM RECREATION AREA: The several fun attractions here include an 18-hole golf course; a water park (Waterworld Safari, (623) 581-1947) with waterslide, wave pool, and sand volleyball court; an oval track for race carts (or "karts"); a paved runway for model airplanes; and a field for ultralight planes and gliders. Entrance at 43rd Avenue and Pinnacle Peak Road. Maricopa County Parks, (602) 506-2930. (D-6)

WHITE TANK MOUNTAIN REGIONAL PARK: Odd name, eh? It comes from the fact that flash floods pouring down the mountainside have scoured out depressions, or "tanks," in the white granite rock. This is the largest park in the Maricopa County park system — 26,692 acres. The mountains rise to 4,083 feet. Seven Hohokam dwelling sites are here, as are the petroglyphs that the Hohokam carved into stone. When it rains enough, a seasonal waterfall spills out, and you can walk the one-mile Waterfall Trail to see it. There are many more

trails in the park for hikers and horseback riders, and lots of picnic and campsites. Vehicle entry fee. The park entrance is on Olive Road/Dunlap Avenue, west of State Route 303. (623) 935-2505. (F-1)

ESTRELLA MOUNTAIN REGIONAL PARK: There's a rodeo arena here and trails popular with horseback riders. Bike riders also love the site, which has many trails over relatively flat land. Other trails are used primarily by hikers seeking excursions from one hour to all day. There are ramadas and picnic sites spread over the park, which has an 18-hole golf course. The history, too, is fascinating. Spanish explorer Coronado may have come through the Estrella Mountains looking for gold, and Father Eusebio Kino was a missionary to the Pima Indians nearly 300 years ago. But archaeological signs show the presence of very early peoples long before these explorations, even before the Hohokam. Vehicle entry fee. Entrance to this Maricopa County park is off Estrella Parkway, south from Interstate 10. (623) 943-3811. (J-2)

(ABOVE) *Sailors especially enjoy the broad, open water of Lake Pleasant, north of Phoenix.* JERRY SIEVE
(RIGHT) *A mountain bike rider makes his way on a single track in the Cave Creek trail system.* MIKE PADIAN
(FAR RIGHT) *Downtown Phoenix and South Mountain, a part of the Phoenix Mountains Preserve, can be seen from the Biltmore golf course.* DICK DIETRICH

PHOENIX MOUNTAINS PRESERVE: At 16,500 acres, South Mountain Park is the largest municipal park in the world and the centerpiece of an unique urban enclave, the Phoenix Mountains Preserve. In all, there are more than 100 miles of trails for hiking and mountain-bike riding in the preserve.

What folks especially like in the park is driving (or hiking or biking) up South Mountain to 2,330-foot Dobbins Overlook, where you're higher than the jets coming in for a landing at Sky Harbor International Airport and the view is all-encompassing. The park preserves several petroglyph locations. Central Avenue in Phoenix goes into the park's north entrance. (602) 495-0222 or 262-7275. (K-7)

The north segment's most popular feature is Squaw Peak — a 1.2-mile climb that also ends with a fantastic overview of the Valley. In a typical non-summer week, about 10,000 people make the hike. Take Glendale Avenue or Lincoln Drive to Squaw Peak Drive and go north about a mile. (602) 262-4889. (G-8)

Rock climbers favor the Camelback Mountain-Echo Canyon Recreation Area. Hiking trails here are very steep, so watch your step. East McDonald Drive and Tatum Boulevard. (602) 256-3110. (G-8)

Christiansen Trail, open to hikers, cyclists, and horseback riders, spans about 15 miles across northern units of the preserve. Access on the west is at Mountain View Park, Seventh Avenue and Cinnabar Avenue. Another access point is North Mountain Park off Seventh Street (F-7). The trail crosses the Dreamy Draw and Squaw Peak recreation areas and on to Tatum Boulevard. Call the Northeast District Ranger Station, (602) 262-7901, for information.

CYCLING: The Phoenix bikeway system runs more than 400 miles, and there's excellent street riding in cities all around the Valley.

A favorite road-bike ride covers 15 miles along the Arizona Canal Diversion Channel. The route is wide and paved, with tunnels underneath most of the busy thoroughfares. One good access point is at Cave Creek Park on Thunderbird Road just east of I-17. In Scottsdale, a multi-use path system with under- and overpasses runs along Indian Bend Wash as it parallels Hayden Road from Indian Bend Road (G-9) to McKellips Road (H-9); Scottsdale bicycle coordinator, (480) 312-2732. Tempe Town Lake offers a lakeside biking loop between Priest Drive and Rural Road/Scottsdale Road; Tempe bicycle coordinator, (480) 350-8810.

For more cycling information, contact these bicycle coordinators: State of Arizona, (602) 712-8010; Maricopa County, (602) 506-1630; Phoenix, (602) 262-1650; Mesa, (480) 644-3824; Glendale, (623) 930-2939; Chandler, (480) 782-3440; and Peoria, (623) 773-7137. For an urban bikeways map call the Maricopa Association of Governments, (602) 254-6308. For more Arizona biking information on the Web, go to *www.azbikeclub.com/*.

GOLF: With more than 170 courses, golf is huge in Phoenix. For a complete guide to golf in Arizona, call the Arizona Golf Association, (602) 944-3035 (*www.azgolf.org/*). This guidebook's Phoenix map (courtesy of Qwest Dex) at Page 130 marks public golf courses with numbered flags. For a listing of course names, go to the map insert (Community Pages, volume A-L) of the Qwest Phoenix Metro Yellow Pages. ◪

Indian Heritage

PRE-HISTORY AND MODERN CULTURES

by Joe Stocker

Besides the institutions sketched below, most Arizona tribes maintain museums and cultural centers. A list of the tribes is at the end of the chapter. Some listings below include a site number and grid coordinates corresponding to the foldout map following Page 130.

THE HEARD MUSEUM: Just a few hours in Phoenix's Heard Museum will expose you to centuries of Native American culture, history, lifestyles, art, and literature. Attend one of its special programs throughout the year — festivals, markets, lectures, and performances — and your experience broadens to include music, dance, humor, and food.

A private, non-profit museum founded in 1929 by Dwight B. and Maie Bartlett Heard, The Heard defines its mission and philosophy as promoting appreciation and respect for native peoples and their cultural heritage. The Heard focuses on the Southwest native peoples, but also embraces aboriginal cultures from regions such as Oceania, Africa, Asia, and the Americas.

Expanded to 130,000 square feet of space with 10 exhibit galleries, library, archives, a multi-purpose auditorium, and displays of traditional and contemporary Native American art, The Heard is the most comprehensive institution of its type. The expansion also added a working artist studio for visiting Native American artists.

Visitors get involved when they explore The Heard.

Consider the interactive exhibit, "Cradles, Corn, and Lizards." It reflects the relationships between the tribes, plants, and animals of Arizona and offers hands-on activities that illustrate these relationships. Two renowned Native American artists designed and created the exhibit's centerpiece, a six-foot-high, multi-sensory wall of interactive delights.

Artists Michael Naranjo, of New Mexico's Santa Clara Pueblo, and Joe Baker, of the Delaware Tribe, worked with sighted and non-sighted children to create the centerpiece. Naranjo, blinded during the Vietnam War, is a noted sculptor who works in bronze. Baker is known for surreal images painted in vibrant colors.

A sampling of The Heard's programs include printmaking demonstrations, the Native American Festival of the Horse, and Hopi pottery workshops.

You'll see a Navajo hogan (traditional tribal dwelling), classic and contemporary Indian jewelry, Navajo weaving demonstrations, the Barry Goldwater and Fred Harvey collections of Hopi kachinas, and a sound-and-image presentation titled "Our Voices, Our Land,"

Overview: The first Southwest natives lived here almost 120 centuries ago. Spear points they used to kill mammoths in what now is southeast Arizona are on display at a Tucson museum. These people formed the Paleo-Indian Culture. As that culture faded, around 5500 B.C., people of the Archaic or Desert Culture moved in. About 2,000 years ago, five cultures — Anasazi, Hohokam, Sinagua, Mogollon, and Salado — had established themselves in the Southwest. As relatively peaceful farmers, artisans, and traders, they thrived for 13 or more centuries and vanished. Many of today's American Indians in Arizona probably come from the lineage of those five cultures. This chapter introduces you to museums, sites, and other institutions that will fascinate you with artifacts, exhibits, and other material preserving and explaining Indian life over 120 centuries.

Heard Museum exhibits and programs help preserve Native American culture, history, lifestyles, and art. (OPPOSITE PAGE) *A hoop dancer performs.* JIM MARSHALL (TOP) *Native American dancers participate in the annual Fiesta Bowl Parade.* DAVID H. SMITH (ABOVE) *The Heard has a campus-like setting.* JERRY SIEVE

Indian Heritage   153

FOLLOWING THE SUN AND MOON
Hopi Katsina Dolls

illustrating the profound relationship between the land and the people of the American Southwest.

The Heard's north branch, with a smaller museum and gallery, is at el Pedregal Festival Marketplace, Scottsdale Road and Carefree Highway (B-9). Gift shops at both museums sell authentic fine art and crafts bought directly from Native American artists.

Admission fee. The main museum is at 22 E. Monte Vista Road off Central Avenue, Phoenix. (602) 252-8840. Web site: *www.heard.org/* (#12, A-3, downtown)

PUEBLO GRANDE MUSEUM: This was the site of a major Hohokam village a thousand years ago, and you can walk along a 0.6-mile trail through the ruin. The Hohokam were the people who showed up in the Salt River Valley around the start of the millennium, stayed for a few hundred years, farmed, dug a sophisticated irrigation system, and then vanished mysteriously. Pueblo Grande is the definitive museum that tells what we know so far of their story.

Here, archaeologists have excavated what they call a platform mound, which is designated a national landmark. Atop the mound are ceremonial chambers and a room that may have been an astronomical observatory. There's a line-of-sight link between this room and the Hole in the Rock in nearby Papago Park (see Page 137).

Archaeologists also have unearthed an ancient ball court and banks of some of the original canals.

A model of a Hohokam home and other exhibits describe Hohokam life and highlight Native American cultures. The cultural park sponsors tours and workshops. Admission fee. 4619 E. Washington St., Phoenix. (602) 495-0901/02; recording, (602) 495-0900; or toll free, (877) 706-4408. (#80, H-8)

HOO-HOOGAM KI MUSEUM: The museum is on the Salt River Pima-Maricopa Indian Community, which includes the Onk Akimel Au-Authm (Pima) and the Xalchidom Pii-pash (Maricopa). The two tribes speak different languages but share similar cultural values.

Constructed of adobe and desert plant materials, as desert dwellings were traditionally built, the museum displays Pima basketry and Maricopa pottery. You can always treat yourself to some of that tasty Indian fry

(ABOVE) *The Heard's kachina exhibit explains the Hopi art of carving masked dolls representing spirits.* KERRICK JAMES (OPPOSITE PAGE, ABOVE) *St. John's Mission serves members of the Gila River Indian Community.* JAMES TALLON (OPPOSITE PAGE, BELOW) *A canopy protects a structure at Casa Grande Ruins National Monument.* JERRY JACKA

bread afterward. No admission charge. Open weekdays year-round; closed weekends. 10005 E. Osborn Road, Scottsdale. (480) 850-8190. (G-10)

GILA RIVER ARTS AND CRAFTS CENTER: The center is both a retail sales outlet for a variety of Indian-made arts and crafts and a museum featuring the ancient Indian arts of pottery and basketry. It is operated by the Gila River Indian Community, which consists of members of the Pima and Maricopa tribes. Next to the museum, Heritage Park contains examples of dwellings of five desert tribes. A restaurant serves some native dishes. Located about 20 minutes south of Phoenix at the Casa Blanca Road exit of Interstate 10. (520) 315-3411.

CASA GRANDE RUINS NATIONAL MONUMENT: The most prominent of the approximately 60 sites here was constructed of desert mud some 650 years ago and later named Casa Grande ("great house" in Spanish) by exploring priest Father Eusebio Kino.

This outstanding product of Hohokam culture and architecture stands four stories high, the largest of all the Hohokam pueblos that have been discovered. A huge modern metal canopy now gracefully covers the pueblo to keep it from being further consumed by the elements.

Nobody quite knows for sure how the Hohokam used the building. Its walls, more than four feet thick at the base, face the four cardinal compass points. Certain wall openings align with the sun and the moon at specific times of the year, such as the summer solstice. Scientists speculate that the Hohokam used these openings to schedule their plantings, harvests, and community celebrations. In 1892, Casa Grande ruins gained legal protection by becoming America's first archaeological preserve. Admission fee. The monument is north of Coolidge on State Route 87, about an hour's drive south of Phoenix. (520) 723-3172.

O'ODHAM TASH: *O'odham* means "people" and *Tash* means "days" in the Tohono O'odham language. Loose

translation: Indian Days. This remarkably popular four-day celebration occurs in February at several locations in the town of Casa Grande, about half-way between Phoenix and Tucson off I-10. Ceremonial dances are a major part of the festival. One of these dances — the Cripple Dance performed by Akimel Tohono basket dancers — tells of a birdlike personage named Hawk who preyed upon the villages until they united to destroy him.

Besides the ceremonial dancing, O'odham Tash includes a powwow, displays of Indian arts and crafts, and a juried show for Indian artisans, plus a parade, rodeo, carnival rides, and a barbecue. This festival has been attracting around 150,000 people in recent years, so expect large crowds and lots of tour buses. Admission fee for most events. (520) 836-4723. Web site: *www.casagrande.com/www/oodham/*

ARIZONA STATE MUSEUM: Essentially an anthropological institution, the museum specializes in materials relating to the prehistoric Hohokam, Mogollon, and Anasazi cultures, as well as the living American Indian cultures of the Southwest. For example, one major display, "Paths of Life," delves into 10 American Indian cultures of Arizona and northwest Mexico: the Seri, Tarahumara, Yaqui, O'odham, Colorado River Yumans, Southern Paiute, Pai, Apache, Hopi, and Navajo.

Among displayed items are 10,000-year-old stone spear points used by Paleo-Indian mammoth hunters in the Ice Age; a replica of a 700-year-old cliff dwelling; and shell and turquoise jewelry made by prehistoric Hohokam farmers.

The museum library has a vast collection of books and papers and is open to the public. The museum is housed in two buildings at the far west end of the University of Arizona campus in Tucson. Admission is free, but parking is either metered or in pay lots. (520) 621-6281. Web site: *www.statemuseum.arizona.edu/*

AMERIND FOUNDATION: Located in southeast Arizona's Texas Canyon, Amerind is a museum, art gallery, and research institute concentrating on the American Southwest's native cultures. The foundation is named "Amerind" as a contraction of "American Indian." Much of the museum's holdings deal with pre-history people and their descendants. Its artifacts number in the tens of thousands, and its library has some 30,000 volumes. Admission fee. Located between Benson and Willcox. Take Exit 318 from Interstate 10 and drive east one mile to the museum's marked turnoff on the left. (520) 586-3666. Web site: *www.amerind.org/*

(LEFT) *An Apache devil dancer performs at O'odham Tash, an annual celebration in Casa Grande.* JAMES TALLON
(ABOVE) *Tohono O'odham youngsters enjoy a stick game.* PETER NOEBELS
(OPPOSITE PAGE) *Oasis O'odham children perform a traditional skipping dance.* EDWARD McCAIN

SMOKI MUSEUM: A Prescott civic group of non-Indians, the Smoki People formed in 1921 to preserve Native American ceremonies. The museum, built in 1935 to resemble a stone pueblo, holds impressive collections of prehistoric and contemporary Native American art and artifacts and spotlights the cultures of the Prescott region, including the prehistoric Fitzmaurice ruin in Prescott Valley's Fain Park. Admission fee. Open weekends year-round; weekdays, April to September. 147 N. Arizona St., Prescott. (520) 445-1230. Web site: *www.prescottaz.com/~smoki/*

MUSEUM OF NORTHERN ARIZONA: This museum focuses on the anthropology, natural history, and art of the Colorado Plateau region, the 130,000 square miles of canyon country covering parts of northern Arizona, Colorado, New Mexico, and Utah. Visitors can learn about prehistoric peoples and the modern cultures of the Hopi, Navajo, Zuni, and other Indian tribes of the plateau. The museum hosts tribal marketplaces and artist demonstrations. Admission fee. Three miles north of Flagstaff on U.S. Route 180. (520) 774-5213. Web site: *www.musnaz.org/*

When You Go

Here's a list of federally recognized Indian tribes in Arizona, the city where they are based or the closest city, tribal phone numbers, and casino information for tribes that operate one:

Ak-Chin Indian Community: Maricopa, (520) 568-2227. Harrah's Ak-Chin Casino, (800) 427-7247.

Cocopah Tribe: Somerton, (520) 627-2102. Cocopah Casino, (800) 237-5687.

Colorado River Indian Tribes (CRIT): Parker, (520) 669-9211. Blue Water Casino, (800) 747-8777.

Fort McDowell Mohave-Apache Indian Community: Fountain Hills, (480) 837-5121. Fort McDowell Gaming Center, (800) 843-3678.

Fort Mohave Indian Tribe: Needles, CA, (760) 629-4591. Spirit Mountain Casino, Mojave Valley, AZ, (520) 346-2000.

Fort Yuma-Quechan Tribe: Yuma, (760) 572-0213.

Gila River Indian Community: Sacaton, (520) 562-1097. Gila River Casino, south of Phoenix, (800) 946-4452.

Havasupai Tribe: Supai, (520) 448-2141.

The Hopi Tribe: Kykotsmovi, (520) 734-2441.

Hualapai Tribe: Peach Springs, (520) 769-2216.

Kaibab Paiute Tribe: Fredonia, (520) 643-7245.

Navajo Nation: Window Rock, (520) 871-6435.

Pascua Yaqui Tribe: Tucson, (520) 883-5000. Casino of the Sun, (520) 883-1700.

Salt River Pima-Maricopa Indian Community: Scottsdale, (480) 850-8056. Casino Arizona at Salt River, (480) 850-7777.

San Carlos Apache Tribe: San Carlos, (520) 475-2361. Apache Gold Casino, Globe, (800) 272-2433.

San Juan Southern Paiute Tribe: Tuba City, (520) 283-4589.

Tohono O'odham Nation: Sells, (520) 383-2028. Desert Diamond Casino, Tucson, (520) 294-7777.

Tonto Apache Tribe: Payson, (520) 474-5000. Mazatzal Casino, (800) 777-7529.

White Mountain Apache Tribe: Whiteriver, (520) 338-4346. Hon Dah Casino, Pinetop, (800) 929-8744.

Yavapai-Apache Tribe: Camp Verde, (520) 567-3649. Cliff Castle Casino, (520) 567-7660.

Yavapai-Prescott Indian Tribe: Prescott, (520) 445-8790. Bucky's Casino, (520) 776-5695; Yavapai Casino, (520) 445-5767.

Index

Bold type indicates photograph.

Adobe Dam Rec. Area, 150
Ajo, 93, 95
Alamo Lake, **79**, 83
Alpine, 53, 55
America West Arena, 130
Amerind Foundation, 103, 156
Antelope House ruin, 29
Antelope Prairie, 20
Anza Historic Trail, 108
Apache Lake, **67**, 149
Apache National Forest, 52, 55
Apache Trail, 147, **147**, 148, **148**
Arizona Center, 131
Arizona Hall of Fame, 133
Arizona Museum of Youth, 143
Arizona Snowbowl, **18**, 18, 23
Arizona-Sonora museum, 114, **115**, 115, 118
Arizona State Museum, 156
Arizona State Parks, 83
Arizona State University, 139, 140
Arizona Temple, 67, 71, 144, **144**
art center, Mesa, 144; Tempe, 138
art museum, Phoenix, 133
Baboquivari Peak, **92**, 92
Bank One Ballpark, 131
Bear Canyon Arch, **124**
Ben Avery gun range, 149
Benson, 97, 98, 103, 156
Besh-ba-Gowah, 55, **68**, 68, 71
Betatakin ruin, **24**, 25, 26
Bill Williams River, **78**, 81, 83
Biosphere II, 118, **118**
birdwatching, 15, **54**, 73, 76, 81, 97, 99, 100, 102, 107, 110, 127, 144
Bisbee, 99, 103
Black Mountains, **86**, 86
Boothill Cemetery, 98
Boyce Thompson arboretum, **67**, 67, 71
Brewery Gulch, 99
Buckskin Mtn park, 82, **83**, 83
buffalo museum, 141
buffalo soldiers, 99
Bullhead City, 87, 89
Bumble Bee, 57, 65
Cabeza Prieta refuge, 93, 94, 95
Cameron Trading Post, 20
Canyon de Chelly, **28**, 28, 29, 31
Canyon Lake, 148, **148**
Cape Royal, **37**, 38
Casa Grande ruins, **155**, 155
Catalina park, 127
Cattail Cove park, 83
Cave Creek trail system, 149, **151**
Century House Museum, 74, 77
Champlin fighter aircraft museum, 144, **145**
Chandler Center for the Arts, 145
Chiricahua monument, 100, **101**, 103

Chiricahua Mountains, **96**, 100
Chloride, 87, **87**, 89
Cleopatra Hill, 60, **61**
Coal Mine Canyon, 30, **31**
Cochise Stronghold, **102**, 102, 103
Coconino National Forest, 14, 15, 18, **23**, 23, 44, 65
Colorado River, 19, 34; Indians, 79; museum, 87, 89
Colossal Cave park, 127
Confederate Air Force Museum, 144
Copper Queen Hotel/Mine, 99
Coronado memorial, 99, 103
Coronado National Forest, 103
Coronado Trail, 52, 54
Cottonwood, 60, 65
Council Rocks petroglyphs, 103
Crossing of the Fathers, 33
Crown King, 57, 65
cycling, 151
Dead Horse Ranch park, 60, **61**, 65
Deer Valley Rock Art Center, 135
Desert View, 19
Devil's Highway, 94
Devine, Andy, 85, 86
Douglas mansion, 61
Douglas, 100, 103
Dragoon Mountains, 103
Eagar, 51
Estrella Mtn. Reg. Park, 150
farmers markets, 144, 145
Flagstaff, 9-11, **10**, 15, 17, 18
Flandrau planetarium, 118
Fleischer Museum, 143
Fort Apache, 49, 50, 55
Fort Bowie, **100**, 100, 103
Fort Huachuca, 99, 103
Fort Verde park, **57**, 57, 65
Fort Yuma, 73
Gadsden Hotel, 100
Gammage Auditorium, 139, **140**
Ganado, 29
ghost towns, 12, 83
Gila River arts and crafts, 155
Gilbert, 144, 145; historical museum, 144
Glen Canyon Dam, **34**, 34, 35, 39
Glendale, 135
Globe, 68, 71
Goldfield, 147
golf, 151
Goulding's Lodge, 28
Grand Canyon Railway, 21, **21**, 23
Grand Canyon, **16**, 17, 19, 23, 36, **37**, 38, 39
Green Valley, 106
Grey, Zane, 41, 43, 47
Hall of Flame, 138
Hance park (Deck Park), 132
Hassayampa preserve, **64**, 65
Havasu wildlife refuge, **78**, 81, 82
Hawley Lake, 50
Heard Museum, **153**, 153, **154**, 154
Heart of Rocks, 100, **101**
Heber, 47

Heritage Square, 132, **133**
history museum, Arizona, 139; Gilbert, 144; Mesa, 144; Phoenix, 132; Scottsdale, 140; Tempe, 139
Hohokam people, 129, 150, 154-156
Holbrook, 44, 47
Homolovi park, **13**, 13, 15
Hoo-Hoogam Ki Museum, 154
Hoover Dam, 88, **89**, 89
Hopi Cultural Center, 30, 31
Hopi mesas, 18, 29, 30
House Rock Valley, 36
Huachuca Mountains, 99
Hualapai Mountain Park, **84**, 85
Hubbell Trading Post, **29**, 29, 30
Hurricane Cliffs, 39
Imperial Dam, 75
Imperial wildlife refuge, **72**, **75**, 75, 77
Indian Bend Wash, 141, 151
Indian tribes list, 157
intaglios, 79
Jacob Lake, 36
Jerome, 60, **61**, 61, 65
Judaica museum, 141
Kaibab National Forest, 23, 39
Kaibab Plateau visitors center, 36
Kartchner Caverns park, 97, 103
Kayenta, 26
Keet Seel ruin, **25**, 26
Kent Springs Trail, 106
King Canyon Trail, **122**, 122, **123**
Kingman, 85, 86, 89
Kitt Peak, **91**, 91, 95
Kofa wildlife refuge, **76**, 76, 77
Lake Havasu City, 81-83
Lake Mary, 15
Lake Mead, **88**, 88, 89
Lake Pleasant Reg. Park, **150**, 150
Lake Powell, **32**, 33, **34**, 34
La Posada, 44, 47
Lavendar open-pit mine, 100
Lees Ferry, 35
library, Phoenix, 132
Little Colorado River, 19, 20
Lomaki ruin, **20**, 20
London Bridge, **80**, 81, 82
Lost Dutchman mine, 67, 135, 147, park, 66, 67, 71, **147**, 147
Lowell Observatory, 11, **11**, 15
Luke Air Force Base, 135
Madera Canyon, **106**, 106, 111, 126, 127, **127**
Marble Canyon, **35**, 35
Martinez Lake, **76**, 76, 77
Mazatzal Mountains, 71
McCormick-Stillman Railroad Park, **137**, **141**, 141
McDowell Mtn. Reg. Park, 149
Mesa, 67, 71, 143-145
Mesa Southwest Museum, 143
Meteor Crater, **13**, 13, 15
Mexico: shopping, 109, 110
military museum, 138
Miller Peak, 99

(LEFT) *Antelope Canyon narrows to a slot on the Kaibito Plateau near Page — hence the description "slot canyon."* RALPH LEE HOPKINS

Index

Mingus Mountain, 61
mining/mineral museum, 134
Mission San Xavier del Bac, **105**, 105, 111, **113**, 113, 118
Mogollon Rim, 14, 43, **43**, **46**
Mohave history/art museum, 86
Montezuma Castle/Well, **56**, 57, 58, 65
Monument Valley, **26**, 26, 27, 28, 31
Morenci, 54, 55
Mormon Lake, 14, 15, 43
Mount Graham, 55
Mount Hopkins, 107
Mount Humphreys, 18
Mount Lemmon, 117, 124, 126, **126**, 127
Mount Lemmon Ski Valley, 124, 127
Mount Wrightson, 106
Museo Chicano, 130
Museum of Northern Arizona, 11, 157
Mystery Castle, **134**, 135
Nakai Indian Center, 44
Nalakihu ruin, 20
Navajo monument, 25, 26, 31
Navajo Mountain, 26
Nogales, 109-111, **110**
North Kaibab Trail, **38**, 38
O.K. Corral, 98
Oak Creek Canyon, **58**, 59
Oatman, 86, 89
Old Oraibi, 30
Old Town Tempe, 138
Old Trails Museum, 44, 47
Old Tucson, 114, **115**, 115, 118
O'odham Day, 95
O'odham Tash, **156**, 156
Organ Pipe monument, **90**, 91, **92**, **93**, 93-95
Orpheum Theater, **129**, 130
ostrich festival, 145
Out of Africa Wildlife Park, 143, **143**
Painted Desert, 14, **45**, 45
Palm Canyon, **76**, 77
Papago Park, 137
Parker, 81, 83; dam, 81
Park of the Canals, 144
Patagonia Lake park, 111
Patagonia-Sonoita refuge, 110, **111**, 111
Patriot park, **129**, 130
Payson, 41, 47; rodeo, **41**
Peña Blanca Lake, 109
Petersen House Museum, **139**, 139
Petrified Forest, **40**, 44, 44, **45**, 45, 47
petroglyphs, **21**, 29, **41**, **88**, 103, **118**, 135, 143, 150
Phoenix, 128-138
Phoenix Civic Plaza, 131
Phoenix Mtns. Preserve, 151
Phoenix Police Museum, 131
Phoenix Zoo, 137, **138**, 138
Phon D. Sutton Rec. Site, 149
Picket Post Mountain, 68
Pimeria Alta Museum, 111
Pine Creek Canyon, 42
Pine, 43
Pine-Strawberry Museum, 47

Pioneer living history museum, 135, **135**
pioneer/military park, 134
Pipe Spring monument, **39**, 39
Pisinimo Trading Post, 92
Powerhouse visitors center, 85
Prescott, 61, 62, 63
Pueblo Grande, 154
Quartermaster Depot, 73, **74**
Quartzsite, **79**, 79
Quechan Indian Tribe, 73, 74
Quitobaquito, **93**, 93, 94
Rails to Trails, 51, 55
railway museum, 145
railroad park, **137**, **141**, 141
Rainbow Bridge, **33**, 33, 39
Ramsey Canyon, 99, 103
Rawhide, 143, **143**
Red Rock park, 65
Rex Allen Days, 102
Rim Road, 44
Rincon Mountains, 123
riparian preserves, 144
Roosevelt Dam/Lake, 69, **70**, 70, 71, 129
Roper Lake park, 54, 55, **55**
Route 66, 44, 85, 86, 89
Sabino Canyon/Creek, **117**, 117, 118, **120**, 121, **123**, 123, 124, **125**, 127
saguaro cactus, **48**, 65, **70**, **91**, **93**, **94**, **117**, **122**, **123**, **136**, **148**, **151**
Saguaro Lake, 149, **149**
Saguaro National Park, 114, 118, 121-123, **122**, 127
St. Mary's Basilica, **132**, 131
St. Thomas Mission, 74
Salado cliff dwellings, 69, **69**
Salt River Project, 132, 139
Salt River rafting, **49**, tubing, 149
San Bernardino refuge, 100, 103
San Carlos Apache Cultural Center, 54, 55
San Francisco Mtns./Pks., **9**, **11**, 14, 15, 18, 20, 30
San Pedro River, 97
Santa Catalina Mountains, 117, 123-126
Santa Cruz River, 105, 107, 114
Santa Rita Mountains, 106, **126**, 126, 127
science museum, 132
Scottsdale, 140-143, 145
Scottsdale Civic Center Mall, 140
Sedona, 58, **58**, 59, **59**, 65
Sells, 92
Sharlot Hall Museum, 62, 65
Shemer Art Center, 138
Show Low, 50
Shrine of St. Joseph, 64
Sierra Vista, 99, 103
Sinagua people, 11, 12, 57, **60**
Sirrine House, 144
Sitgreaves National Forest, 47
Skull Valley, 63, **64**
Slaughter Ranch, 100, 103
Slide Rock park, 58, **59**, 65
Smoki Museum, 62, 65, 157
snow skiing, 15, 18, **18**, 23, 50, 51, 53, 55,

117, 124, 127
Sonoita, **104**, **110**, 110
Sonoran Desert, **90**, 91, 115, 123
Spider Rock, 29
Springerville, 51, 52
Standing Cow ruin, 29
State Capitol Museum, 133, **134**
Strawberry, 43; schoolhouse, **43**, 43
Summerhaven, 117
Sunrise Park Resort, **50**, 50, 51
Sunset Crater volcano, 20, 22, **23**, 23
Superstition Mountains, **66**, 67, 147-149
Swansea, 83
Taliesin West, 143
Telephone Pioneer Museum, 133
Tempe, 138-140, 145; town lake, 138, 151
Titan Missile Museum, 105, 111
Tohono O'odham, 91, 92, 95, 113, **156**, 156, 157
Tombstone, 97, **98**, 98, 103
Tonto National Forest, 71, **148**, 148, 149
Tonto monument, **69**, 69, 71
Tonto Natural Bridge, **42**, 42, 47
Topock Gorge, 82, **82**
Tubac, 107, **108**, 108, 111
Tucson Mtn. Park, 114; mtns, 122
Tucson city map, 119
Tumacacori park, 108, 111
Tuzigoot monument, **60**, 60, 65
Usery Mtn. Rec. Area, 149
Verde Canyon Railroad, **60**, 60, 65
Verde Valley, 57
Vermilion Cliffs, **33**, 35, **36**, 36
Vision Gallery, 145
Walnut Canyon, 11, **12**, 12, 15
Whipple Observatory, **107**, 107, 111
Whiskey Row, **62**, 62
White House ruin, 28
White Mtn. Apache Cultural Center, 49, 55
White Tank Mtn. Reg. Park, 150
Whiteriver, 50
Wickenburg, **64**, 64, **65**, 65
Wildlife World Zoo, 135
Willcox, 102, 103
Windsor Beach, 83
Windy Point, 117, 126, **126**
Winslow, 14, 44
Winsor Castle, **39**, 39
Wukoki ruin, 21
Wupatki monument, 20, 21, **22**, 23
Yarnell, 64
Yuma Crossing, 73, **74**, 77
Yuma Territorial Prison, **73**, 73, 75, 77
xeriscape gardens, 137, **137**, 144, 145

(RIGHT) *Joshua trees line the Virgin River Canyon in Beaver Dam Wilderness.* JACK DYKINGA